# A Few Short Plays to Save the World

Steve Harper

Edited by Shawn René Graham
Introduction by Ty Jones

LAUGHING PANDA
PRESS

# CONTENTS

# FOREWORD

Welcome to *A Few Short Plays to Save the World*.

Playwright Steve Harper and I have knowxn each other since our days at The American Repertory Theatre Institute at Harvard University twenty-five years ago. Neither of us could have known then where we would end up in the worlds of film, television and theatre. Steve was a fine actor then, but became an excellent writer. I was in the Dramaturgy program and still work as a dramaturg to this day. We have collaborated many times over the years and I am honored to introduce actors, readers and writers to this plethora of output spanning two decades.

This anthology is a collection of new plays to not only be read and studied, but also to be produced. I know that Steve's impetus to start writing began because he needed and wanted to see a representation of himself and his world not often afforded to him as an actor. As the late Toni Morrison said, "If there's a book that you want to read, but it hasn't been written yet, then you must write it." And, so it goes with Steve and his plays.

The feast of plays you are about to enjoy are diverse and explore cross-sections of race, class and politics, the wonders of love, the discovery of the forgotten and the complexity of human relations.

The plays have one unifying theme. They are topical with strong, dramatic construction and are a wonderful display of what it is like to live at the intersection of a world in which one is a creative, a friend, a lover, a politician or a worker in the world of the United States in the 21st century. Divided into sections, these 17 plays from 4 minutes to 34 minutes long, contain characters that are innovative, provocative and widely diverse. Each section is a testament to the times in which we are currently living. The people seem ordinary at first, but they are on a path to discover extraordinary truths. I will highlight some of them here, but leave it to you, the reader, to investigate further.

In *Many Happy Returns* a grumpy Abbud receives an unusual return item in a box from a mysterious woman on Christmas Eve. This play combines realism with the supernatural that forces one to reveal one's vulnerabilities in order to bring two people closer together.

*Actual Cost* is about B.T. and Iyana, an interracial couple, on their way to a wedding when they encounter Michael, a queer, black homeless man. When Michael asks for a donation, Iyana wants to give and B.T. doesn't. They didn't know what they didn't know about each other. Their perspectives on race, class and money, topics that so often divide us, hinder the ability to express empathy to those that need it most.

*The Political Machine* is a strong portrait of our current state of politics in the United States. Betty Jefferson watches the presidential returns with her husband, Fred, terrified about the fact that one of the candidates isn't even human and increasingly aware that Fred doesn't seem to object to that fact.

*Give Me the Card* is a satirical take on how to define Blackness. In a searingly, witty argument, a black man gets summoned by a Higher Authority and accused of not being black enough. The play explodes the idea that Black people are a monolith and exposes the harsh realities of a character that floats between the expectations of the Black community and his true self-identity. The Black card is a metaphor for the precariousness of Black lives in America.

The words and tools of imagery in *Abstract Purple* capture the struggles of a city-dwelling teenager. When Rosa runs away from home and takes shelter in a Harlem apartment, she didn't bargain for the fact that the place is occupied by Mary, an elderly woman who is facing her own mortality. The subtle and powerful writing unveils an unlikely union between two people and a much needed message about honoring multi-generation connections to one another. Lessons can and should go both ways. Growth as a person should be continuous.

*A Few Short Plays to Save the World* is ultimately an anthology of hope. The plays aforementioned and the twelve others are a testament to an artist who persevered, told the stories he wanted to tell and shared a perspective much needed in the American theatre. Whether you are an educator, a director, a performer or a writer there is much to savor in Steve Harper's words. There is richness to celebrate in these pages. May these plays be of use to those in need of these unique representations and may they flourish on stages everywhere.

Ms. Shawn René Graham
Director of Literary Programs
The Classical Theatre of Harlem

# INTRODUCTION

Romare Bearden, recognized as one of the most important visual artists of our time, said that "art is born out of necessity". Whether you are an actor or a writer, the urge to respond to a world before you is a vulnerable, brave endeavor. The act of doing it is one thing; sharing it with the world is an altogether different beast.

In my journey as an actor, I recall on several occasions how my fellow thespians would often look to each other for texts, scenes or monologues that would showcase our work. To this day, I would wager that many of us would recycle the same pieces to the point that casting directors would find them stale, hackneyed and routine. Full transparency, I worked in several casting offices as a reader and witnessed how predictable the choices would be – especially for Black actors and actresses.

Given the challenges ANYONE, let alone actors of color must endure to make a life in the arts, I would find myself wondering about this lack of variety in choices. Many of the artists who came into the room were from the highest profiled institutions, they were indeed talented – surely conversations were had about their choice of material, whether it was for a monologue or a showcase. Something was missing.

Cynicism can always find a way to distract an artist, and at times it can be paralyzing. Part of the work of being an artist is to essentially, solve problems. Take whatever is before you, go into your wheelhouse, employ the necessary tools, collaborate and make a choice. An empty page, a blank canvas, an empty stage – is permission to create.

Steve Harper's Short Play Anthology is a creation of something special. It solves a problem. There was a blank canvas ready to be filled in, as if the writer heard the countless voices of artists – young, distinguished, vulnerable – with an insatiable desire for material that is inclusive, interesting, funny, insightful, current – and made a choice to do what artists do, create.

You need a two hander? No problem. What about Asian or Indian characters? It's there. Strong female leads? Check. Latinx, Black, non-descript, pathos, youth, wisdom, inside baseball, out of this world humor – check, check, check.

Anyone who asks for suggestions on practical ways to work on one's craft, whether they are veterans or recently inspired to explore this creative world, I can now say there is a universal body of work that is precisely what the 20 year-old version of me ordered.

This anthology is necessary. Born out of a necessity. Thank you, Steve.

Ty Jones
Producing Artistic Director
The Classical Theatre of Harlem

# LOVE

*"Love takes off the mask we fear we cannot live without and know we cannot live within."*

*-James Baldwin*

# First Encounter

# First Encounter

*An upscale restaurant. Bob and Jessica sit together, both nicely dressed. They look at menus. Bob puts his menu down and stares at Jessica.*

JESSICA: Everything looks good.

BOB: Especially you.

*She looks at him. Puts her menu down.*

JESSICA: You're not so bad either. (beat) I don't know how long you've been doing the online thing –

BOB: Too long –

JESSICA: Me too! You never know who you're going to end up with.

BOB: Tell me about it.

JESSICA: No one ever looks like their picture – they're either older or fatter or shorter – or they're missing teeth.

BOB: Or they're idiots. Can't string two sentences together. Aren't up on the latest current events.

JESSICA: Right! And just talking with you when we were waiting for the table – you're – great conversationally.

BOB: You too.

JESSICA: Thanks. It's one of my gifts. (beat) And you seem really smart. You went to Harvard.

BOB: And Princeton.

JESSICA: Nice. And – frankly – you're better looking than your photo.

BOB: So are you.

*Bob smiles at Jessica. They turn back to their menus.*

JESSICA: What do you think you'll have?

BOB: It's difficult to concentrate on food, actually. (beat) But - I'm thinking of the Linguini.

JESSICA: So am I!

BOB: I was also thinking of -

BOB: - the steak.

JESSICA: The steak!

JESSICA: Jinx! I think I'll have the steak.

> *They both put the menus down.*

JESSICA: We talked about so many things online - I feel like I know you already.

BOB: Me too.

JESSICA: But - what about your work? I've told you everything about the district attorney's office. In fact my friends ask me to shut up about it, I talk about work so much. What about you?

BOB: You want me to tell you to shut up about it?

JESSICA: No - you haven't told me much about what you do. You said "sales" and "fundraising".

BOB: Right.

JESSICA: Who do you work for?

BOB: Myself.

> *Beat. Bob looks for the waiter.*

JESSICA: You don't want to talk about it?

BOB: No, it's - I like talking about it. I just - sometimes other people don't like talking about it.

JESSICA: I'm not other people. What do you sell?

BOB: Lemonade. (beat) I have a stand. On the street. Dollar a glass.

JESSICA: You make your own lemonade and sell it? By yourself? Like – the way kids do?

BOB: My stuff is much better than any pre-pubescent. I have a secret recipe. And regular customers. My lemonade is superb. And I like selling it.

JESSICA: OK. I'd – like to – try it – some time. You – make money doing that?

BOB: Of course. (beat) And I do fundraising.

JESSICA: (joking) On the street?

BOB: Sometimes. But also on the subway. You know –

JESSICA: You mean like – no – how do you mean?

BOB: I – get on a train and I carry a sign and a coffee can with change in it. I – shake my can and I give a – verbal pitch for funds.

JESSICA: You beg.

BOB: I fundraise.

*Beat.*

JESSICA: Do you – say you're – homeless? Do you lie? Because you told me you have a condo.

BOB: I do have a condo. And I don't lie – I just explain that I'm – not working a regular job and that I'm hungry – because sometimes I am –

JESSICA: When people on the subway with a sign and a can full of change say they're hungry –

BOB: I mention my Ivy League credits and I say that others are – less fortunate than I. I tell the truth and people are generous. I make a good living between the lemonade and the –

JESSICA: Begging.

# First Encounter

BOB: Fundraising.

JESSICA: A person like you - smart and good looking - I mean - where's the security in lemonade?

BOB: Lemons aren't going anywhere.

JESSICA: And neither are the subways huh?

BOB: This is why I don't tell people.

JESSICA: There are people out there who NEED charity. Who need help. You're not one of those people.

BOB: People give me money. Am I supposed to say "No thank you?"

JESSICA: You seemed like a nice guy.

BOB: I am a nice guy, that's why people drink my lemonade. That's why they fill my can. And sometimes - I sing, play my Ukulele and dance. The crowds love it!

JESSICA: Wait - I've seen you. On the train - Oh my god! This is - you're - not right. I'm leaving. (beat) You call that dancing?

BOB: Everyone enjoys what I do!

JESSICA: At least I have a real job - a desk - benefits and a 401K. What do you have?

BOB: The ability to set my own hours. A tax-free income. And work that I love. (beat) That I really, really love.

*Jessica stands.*

BOB: Can I email you?

*Jessica screams and storms out.*

BOB: Is that a maybe?

*Lights.*

5

# Many Happy Returns

# Many Happy Returns

*Lights up on a counter at a department store. A big sign:
Holiday Returns, hangs above the counter. We hear Christmas
music. Abbud, 30s, Iranian American, is at the counter, looking
bored. An elegant White Woman approaches carrying an
unmarked cardboard box.*

ABBUD: Can I help you?

WOMAN: Excuse me?

ABBUD: Yes?

WOMAN: What happened to "Welcome to Cunningham's. Happy
Holidays! How may I help you?"?

ABBUD: Yes, right. Sorry. Welcome to Cunningham's. Happy
Holidays! How may I help you?

WOMAN: You should work on that. More enthusiasm. I know you
don't believe. In anything. And you've been depressed. But you're good
at pretending. So do it. Do I look familiar to you? Do you know who I
am?

ABBUD: I - um - Are you - on TV?

WOMAN: Certainly not! You don't know me.

ABBUD: I don't. No.

WOMAN: That's a shame really. I'm Margaret. Margaret Cunningham.

ABBUD: Oh. Oh my god. I'm - wow. I'm sorry I didn't recognize you.
I don't think I've seen you in the store before.

MARGARET: I'm here a lot.

ABBUD: Of course. Yes. You must be. I just - maybe I don't work a
lot. Mrs. Cunningham -

MARGARET: Ms.

ABBUD: Ms. Cunningham. I'm sorry I didn't realize. How may I help you?

MARGARET: I want to return this.

ABBUD: Of course.

*He takes the box and puts it on the counter. Goes to open it.*

MARGARET: Don't open it.

ABBUD: I have to – in order to process the return.

MARGARET: Wait until I leave. I don't want to see it. It's from Charles – my ex-husband. He knows I don't want gifts from him. I don't want reminders of how I wasted 20 years of my life. He goes out of his way to send me things I don't need.

ABBUD: That sounds awful.

MARGARET: It sucks.

ABBUD: Sounds sucky.

MARGARET: Good for you. So, when I walk away, you can open the box and scan the barcode – or however it works and process the refund to whatever card he charged it on and restock it and that will be that.

ABBUD: Yes. Sure.

*She studies him for several beats. A thorough evaluation.*

MARGARET: Alright, Abbud. You carry on. Have a good evening.

ABBUD: Thank you, Ms. –

*She's gone. Abbud looks after her.*

ABBUD: Weird. (beat) How did she know my name?

*He opens the box. Pulls out another cardboard box. There's writing on this one, but no logo or anything. Abbud examines it. Shrugs. Pulls out his price scanner and scans. A WRONG*

*ANSWER sound, erupts, like on a game show. Abbud scans again. Same sound. He tries again. Same. Abbud picks up a phone on the counter. Dials.*

ABBUD: Erica? (beat) Is she there? (beat) Well, I could use some help. At returns? (beat) Ok. Well, when she's done. It's – it's for one of the Cunninghams, so. (beat) No, they're not still here. But – (beat) Ok.

*Hangs up. Stares at the box again. Grabs his cell phone. Dials.*

ABBUD: Hey. (beat) I know you don't – (beat) I could – use some help. (beat) Yes, a work thing. (beat) Can't you take a break? Isn't there someone else at the counter with you? It's store business. (beat) I did call and Erica is handling – something. (beat) Ok! I wouldn't call if I didn't – (beat) Thanks. Really.

*Hangs up. Stares at the box. Justin, a young black man, appears. He's annoyed.*

JUSTIN: Why are you calling me?

ABBUD: I told you. I need help.

JUSTIN: Now, you want my help. Now you can't do whatever it is without me.

ABBUD: I didn't say I was helpless.

JUSTIN: But you need help.

ABBUD: Yeah.

JUSTIN: With?

ABBUD: This –

*He shoves the box toward Justin. Justin looks at it. Laughs.*

JUSTIN: What is it?

ABBUD: It's what it says.

*Justin reads the box.*

JUSTIN: It says "Enlightenment".

*Abbud gestures: yeah.*

JUSTIN: In a box?

ABBUD: I don't know how it works.

JUSTIN: This is what you need help with?

ABBUD: It's a return from a Cunningham.

JUSTIN: Oh! Really? Who?

ABBUD: Do you know the Cunninghams? There are a lot of them.

JUSTIN: Yeah. Not really.

ABBUD: Me neither. But - they're like royalty.

JUSTIN: Duh!

ABBUD: Anyway, I'm supposed to process this.

JUSTIN: And -

*Abbud scans the box. That nasty sound again.*

JUSTIN: Give me that.

*Abbud hands it over. Justin scans. Same sound. They stare at the box.*

ABBUD: Maybe we don't sell this.

JUSTIN: Enlightenment?

ABBUD: Exactly. Which means I can't process the return. Which means, I can't do what Ms. Cunningham asked. Which is bad.

JUSTIN: Maybe she didn't get it from here.

ABBUD: Her ex-husband got it.

JUSTIN: Oh shit.

ABBUD: Yeah. So, I can't give it back to her. I can't have her paged or try to find her in order to give her bad news like that.

JUSTIN: That's a problem.

ABBUD: Told ya. What do I do?

JUSTIN: You'd think she'd know what they sell at her own store.

ABBUD: You'd think.

JUSTIN: It's so ironic that you want my help now.

ABBUD: Can you not –

JUSTIN: After all, you needed your independence.

ABBUD: Yeah, ok, get it over with.

JUSTIN: You couldn't deal with me anymore.

ABBUD: Never said that.

JUSTIN: That's how it felt. You didn't like my music. My friends.

ABBUD: Some of them were fine.

JUSTIN: I snored.

ABBUD: You do!

JUSTIN: My Farsi wasn't good.

ABBUD: I never asked you to learn Farsi.

JUSTIN: My pronunciation was off.

ABBUD: It was!

JUSTIN: You stopped caring about me.

ABBUD: That's not what –

JUSTIN: You had to be on your own. You said that, right? (beat) Right? Right. (beat) So I avoid you for months. Choose different shifts. Steer clear. And now – Christmas Eve – when we're both here – Oh Holy Night. Your favorite shift.

ABBUD: I hate this shift.

JUSTIN: People are too cheery. I know. On this night of all nights, you need my help. To do your stupid little job.

ABBUD: I deserve all that.

JUSTIN: Yes. You. Do.

ABBUD: I never said I didn't care about you.

JUSTIN: Tomato. To-mah-to.

ABBUD: You don't have to help me if you don't want to.

 *Beat.*

JUSTIN: Look it up – by the number.

ABBUD: Yes! Right. Duh.

 *Abbud finds a code on the box. Types in the number on the register. A different sound – equally bad.*

ABBUD: Nothing.

JUSTIN: Then we don't sell it. No enlightenment at Cunningham's.

 *He chuckles.*

ABBUD: It's not funny.

JUSTIN: It kinda is.

ABBUD: What do I – ?

JUSTIN: Wait.

*Justin pulls out his cell. He types. Waits. Waits. Sees a result.*

JUSTIN: Nothing's coming up.

ABBUD: So - no one sells this? It doesn't exist? How is that -

JUSTIN: I don't know. How could this not be a product?

ABBUD: We should open it.

JUSTIN: Can't do that.

ABBUD: I'll pay the restocking fee.

JUSTIN: It's from her ex. Right? Could be a bomb.

*Abbud puts his ear to the box. Justin does, too.*

JUSTIN: I don't hear anything.

ABBUD: Nope.

JUSTIN: So what's in there?

ABBUD: Enlightenment. No assembly required.

JUSTIN: Bomb sold separately.

*They share a smile.*

ABBUD: Let's open it.

JUSTIN: I'm not getting fired over a box.

ABBUD: Ms. Cunningham's ex is playing some kind of game on her. We get to the bottom of it. Then we're heroes. Then they love us.

JUSTIN: Or it's a bomb and it explodes. And then we die.

ABBUD: That's so morbid. (beat) You're not curious about what's in here?

JUSTIN: Yeah, kinda. You got a scissors?

*Abbud excitedly starts searching the returns station. Justin, impatient, joins him on the other side to search. It's a bit of a production. Erica, an Asian woman, walks up in a Mrs. Claus outfit. She stands there watching.*

ABBUD: Oh! Whoa! Hi, Erica.

JUSTIN: What? Oh, Erica. Hi.

ERICA: Ho ho ho. What is happening here? Why are the two of you in the same hemisphere?

ABBUD: I needed help.

ERICA: Which is why you call me.

ABBUD: You had an emergency.

ERICA: Yeah. It's over. Mrs. Claus took ill. I stood in. Is there something going on with you two that I should know about?

ABBUD: No.

JUSTIN: No.

ABBUD: It's work related. I needed help because –

JUSTIN: – he's trying to process this return.

ABBUD: From one of the Cunninghams. But we don't sell this.

*He pushes the box toward Erica. Erica looks at it.*

ERICA: What the hell?

JUSTIN: Exactly. Doesn't scan. It's not in the system.

ERICA: Which Cunningham?

JUSTIN: Do you know the Cunninghams?

ERICA: It's my job to know the Cunninghams. Of course.

JUSTIN: Dumb question.

*Abbud shoots Justin a look.*

ABBUD: Margaret.

ERICA: Come again?

ABBUD: Margaret.

ERICA: You saw Margaret Cunningham? Tonight?

ABBUD: She gave me this box.

ERICA: No, she didn't.

ABBUD: She did.

JUSTIN: Why didn't she?

ERICA: Cause she's no longer with us.

JUSTIN: Whaaaat?

ABBUD: Noooooo.

ERICA: Yeah. She's - It's been a few years.

ABBUD: Oh, wait a minute waitaminute.

ERICA: She was really nice. Well, she liked me. She would give gifts to employees - especially at holiday time. Couldn't have been her.

ABBUD: She said she was her. She gave me this box.

ERICA: Where did she say it was from?

ABBUD: Her ex-husband - Charles.

ERICA: She never married. (beat) Ooooh. She gave it to you. It's your gift. Your holiday gift. From the ghost of the department store. That's cute. That's weird. Get a scissors.

> *Abbud and Justin scramble. Erica joins them behind the counter. Abbud pops up with one in his hand.*

ABBUD: Scissors!

ERICA: Gimme.

ABBUD: No. I should open it. She gave it to me. It's – technically my gift. If it's not a return, I mean.

ERICA: And it's not a bomb.

ABBUD: It's not a bomb.

JUSTIN: It's not a bomb.

ABBUD: Doesn't tick. You're on board with opening this, right? We won't get in trouble.

ERICA: No. Open the damn thing.

> *Abbud cuts the top of the box. Then the sides. Erica and Justin lean over as Abbud pulls the flaps back. LIGHT POURS OUT OF THE BOX, bathing their faces and brightening the store. All three are stupefied. Abbud closes the box.*

ABBUD: Holy –

JUSTIN: It's beautiful.

ERICA: Miraculous.

ABBUD: I don't think I've ever felt so –

JUSTIN: Peaceful.

ERICA: Relaxed.

JUSTIN: Amazing.

# Many Happy Returns

*Abbud takes a deep breath and has a MOMENT OF TRUTH.*

ABBUD: I broke up with you because I was afraid. I wasn't good enough for you. I thought I didn't deserve to have someone as special as you are.

JUSTIN: What? But you were mean.

ABBUD: I didn't mean to be mean I didn't know what to do. I lied. I didn't object to any of things about you. I just thought you deserved better than me. And I didn't deserve... I - a lot of the time I don't feel - lovable.

*A beat as that statement lands.*

ERICA: What's happening?

JUSTIN: I didn't want better than you.

ABBUD: You didn't?

JUSTIN: I don't.

ERICA: That's really sweet. It's almost too sweet. Like I'm gonna be sick.

JUSTIN: Don't.

ABBUD: You need a tissue?

ERICA: I'm fine.

ABBUD: I'm sorry.

JUSTIN: You should be sorry. But - I'm - well - thanks.

*They stare at each other a moment.*

ERICA: Wow. That's some box!

ABBUD: I gotta get out of here.

ERICA: Why?

ABBUD: I just - I can't keep this to myself: this - box. This honesty, this sense of relief, joy - it has to be shared.

JUSTIN: That's so generous.

ABBUD: Right? Come with me.

JUSTIN: Really?

ERICA: I can't leave. Not looking like this. Besides, I'm the supervisor on duty.

ABBUD: I wasn't really asking you.

ERICA: Oh. Well, I'll get someone to cover your post. And yours. Go.

*Abbud takes Erica's Santa hat.*

ABBUD: Thanks, Erica.

ERICA: Merry Christmas.

ABBUD: Happy Holidays.

JUSTIN: Merry everything.

*Abbud and Justin walk out holding the box between them.*

ERICA: Ms. Cunningham? Are you out really here? Cause, if you've got an extra box -

*Lights.*

# This is Now

# This is Now

*Lights up.*

THE CAR

*Grace (20s) sits next to Kevin (20s). Alice (40s) is behind them.*

KEVIN: This seems pretty way out. Off the beaten track, whatever. You sure we're going in the right direction?

GRACE: Yeah, this is the way. Thought you said you got the heat fixed.

KEVIN: I didn't. How do you know this is the way if you've never been here before?

GRACE: I got directions.

KEVIN: But you're not even looking at a map or whatever.

GRACE: Don't worry about it. You should have worried about the heat.

KEVIN: We're out here in the woods –

GRACE: It's not the woods.

KEVIN: Are there black people out here? You better hope we don't get stopped and pulled over and arrested and beaten and robbed.

GRACE: Will you shut up? We're fine.

KEVIN: This better not be KKK country.

GRACE: Kevin, it's upstate New York!

ALICE: Turn left here.

GRACE: Turn left here.

THE HOUSE

*Tate (50s) sits in the living room shuffling cards. Alice sits with him.*

ALICE: You know I can't play.

TATE: I don't believe you.

ALICE: I was always terrible at card games. And you know I'm not allowed to touch anything.

TATE: So I'll deal for you. And I'll play your hand. And I'll just look at you.

ALICE: For how long?

TATE: As long as they'll let me.

ALICE: There's a car outside.

*There's a knock at the door.*

TATE: Did you do that? Who is it?

ALICE: I'm a ghost. Not a psychic.

TATE: I'm not getting it. (beat) Nick! (beat)

ALICE: He's in the bathroom.

*Tate smiles, shakes his head. Goes to the door. Alice exits. Tate lets Grace in. They stare at each other.*

TATE: Grace?

GRACE: Mr. Hendrickson.

TATE: Tate.

GRACE: Tate.

TATE: Nick - was Nick expecting you?

GRACE: No. Um -

TATE: Nice to see you.

GRACE: This is my cousin, Kevin.

TATE: Tate Hendrickson.

KEVIN: Sure, yeah. I know you. Read your stuff. Cool stuff.

TATE: Some of it I still like.

GRACE: Kevin's my ride.

TATE: You came from the city?

GRACE: I wanted to - say - I'm sorry to hear about your - cancer.

TATE: Thanks. At least it's early. They'll get it all out if I'm lucky. I'm usually lucky.

GRACE: I've heard that about you.

*She hands him a box of candy.*

GRACE: This is for you. I hope it's the kind you like.

TATE: Uh, thanks. (beat) Nick's here. I'll get Nick.

GRACE: Um. Actually -

TATE: Yes?

GRACE: Kevin, could you -

KEVIN: Uh - yeah. You got a bathroom?

TATE: Through there.

*Kevin exits. Grace and Tate stare at each other. Nick bounds in.*

NICK: Hey, whose car is that out front? (beat) Hey.

GRACE: Hey.

NICK: What are you doing here? Everything OK?

GRACE: Yeah, fine.

*Nick holds out his arms for a hug. Beat. Grace hugs him.*

NICK: Is that your car? I thought you couldn't drive.

GRACE: My cousin's. (beat. To Tate.) I had - traffic - issues.

NICK: Surprised you came up - we just saw each other.

GRACE: Yeah. Um. But - you said your dad was sick and - I haven't seen him - in years.

NICK: You're here to see dad? Why? (beat) Dad?

TATE: Got me.

GRACE: Well - Remember when you introduced me to your father?

GRACE: We went up to the University -

NICK: and we all had dinner.

TATE: Oh god. (beat) I - Nick - I -

NICK: What?

GRACE: He made a pass at me.

TATE: I did.

NICK: What?

TATE: It was years ago - I was drunk - it was - stupid.

GRACE: No - it -

NICK: What do you mean no? Did he or not?

GRACE: He - yes. But - it - wasn't stupid. It was - actually - kind of sweet. At the time I was - I got really angry at you. But - he was lonely.

*Beat.*

GRACE: You were lonely.

TATE: Alice had just died.

GRACE: And that was back when you were drinking and you're not anymore.

TATE: I'm not anymore. How do you know that?

GRACE: And I've been thinking about you.

NICK: About my father?

GRACE: Nick. We're not together.

NICK: We could be.

GRACE: No.

*Kevin enters.*

NICK: And who the fuck are you?

KEVIN: Who the fuck are you?

GRACE: My cousin.

TATE: Grace - I haven't seen you in -

GRACE: I know. I know. But, long before I met you, Tate, before I met Nick. I read all your stuff. *The Holiday Keepers* - everything. And - I was really - I was - actually glad you - grabbed me - under the table.

NICK: God!

GRACE: Because I was - have been - interested in you - for - I'm really sorry Nick - for a very long time.

KEVIN: You have?

NICK: What a load of crap. Get out - get the fuck out -

KEVIN: Don't talk to her like that.

NICK: What are you going to do?

TATE: Stop it, both of you.

GRACE: I just – I just wanted to see you face to face, Tate. I thought with the hospital and – I just wanted to tell you. (beat) I'll go.

NICK: This is too fucking weird.

TATE: Shut up. (beat) I'm – really flattered. (beat) And – You've kinda been on my mind too.

NICK: Oh please!

TATE: Yeah. You have. Nick's been talking about you. And you know – I've been thinking – about you. It's kind of amazing that you – It's good to see you. But we – shouldn't –

*Alice returns.*

GRACE: No?

ALICE: Tate. You don't have to send her away. I can't stay. We both know that.

NICK: Dad. I think you should ask her to leave. I will if you don't. (To Grace.) He doesn't need this.

KEVIN: He didn't quite say that.

TATE: Maybe Nick's right. You better go.

KEVIN: Oh. Well that's pretty clear. But I was kinda hoping you might read one of my short stories and give me some feedback.

GRACE: Kevin.

KEVIN: That's the whole reason I drove you up here! (beat) Can I leave some and maybe you could give me notes or whatever?

GRACE: Kevin!

KEVIN: All right!

NICK: You better go.

ALICE: I have to go.

TATE: Now?

ALICE: Yes.

*Beat.*

TATE: Thanks.

GRACE: For what?

TATE: For - you know. (beat) Look - If I make it out of this surgery alive, maybe - can I call you?

NICK: Dad! (beat) I'm not taking you to the hospital. Forget it. (beat) I'll be upstairs.

*Nick exits.*

TATE: Kevin. Leave your stuff. I'll take a look.

KEVIN: Thanks. Cool. Wow. Really? I didn't think you would. (beat) It's in the car.

*He exits. Tate smiles at Grace.*

TATE: Thank you.

*They hug. Tate kisses her on the cheek. Looks at her. Then he looks over his shoulder at Alice, who is giving him a look. Beat.*

TATE: What?

*Lights.*

# Iggie Imagines Marriage

*A clock chimes a short tune before striking one o'clock. Lights up on a small private room in a church. The room is simple, with traces of religious elegance: carpeted kneelers, a paschal candle, altar clothes neatly hanging from a rack. Against one wall a window looks out onto the street. It is snowing outside.*

*Iggie, 30s and fabulous, is seated in the center of the room with his head held back and his nose pinched. Matthew, 30s and attractive with classical features, stands over him. Both men wear tuxedos.*

MATTHEW: Did it stop?

*Beat. Iggie doesn't move.*

IGGIE: I don't know.

MATTHEW: You have to un-pinch your nose to check.

*He un-pinches and sits up slowly.*

IGGIE: I think so. I think it stopped.

MATTHEW: Thank God.

*Iggie puts his glasses on. He smiles at Matthew.*

IGGIE: What would I do without you?

MATTHEW: You'd still be pinching your nose. No – actually – it's Saturday – one o'clock – you'd be shopping – where?

IGGIE: Today's Man.

MATTHEW: Of course. Checking out today's men.

IGGIE: What else?

*Matthew runs to a wastebasket and proceeds to vomit.*

IGGIE: There's always puking in a wastebasket. Have I told you how lovely that is?

# Iggie Imagines Marriage

MATTHEW: Be supportive.

IGGIE: I know you're nervous. I just thought you were through with that. You have an audience waiting.

MATTHEW: Not to mention a fiancée. How's the crowd? Check.

*Iggie goes to the door and looks out.*

IGGIE: Nzinga seems to be doing stand up in the back of the church.

MATTHEW: Nothing phases her.

IGGIE: But your family looks like they got bumped from the same flight.

MATTHEW: That's how they usually look. (beat) Remember Cooper's wedding?

IGGIE: Of course, I caught the bouquet.

MATTHEW: Pam caught the bouquet.

IGGIE: You held me back.

MATTHEW: They had that great slide show at the reception. We don't have anything like that.

IGGIE: It was tacky. Who cares what the bride and groom looked like in the primary grades? Today will be a lot more fun – and memorable. (beat) You've got me haven't you?

MATTHEW: That means I've got more to worry about.

IGGIE: Try worrying about the fact that you're in here and the wedding party is out there.

*Matthew crosses to look out a window.*

MATTHEW: I don't get how people can walk around without hats in the snow.

IGGIE: They can't all have your fashion sense.

MATTHEW: This is not about fashion – it's about warmth.

IGGIE: Tune in next time to 'Chapeau Chat' when we'll discuss after-wedding bonnets. We really should start.

MATTHEW: One more minute.

*Matthew grabs his iPod. Puts the headphones on.*

IGGIE: Matt – buddy –

*Iggie starts scratching.*

IGGIE: See what you did?

MATTHEW: What? I'm listening to Sports Talk.

IGGIE: You can do that any time. It's a podcast!

MATTHEW: It relaxes me –

IGGIE: Any minute your mother's going to charge in here, wrap her Rosary beads around your neck and pull you out onto the stage.

MATTHEW: It's an altar, not a stage.

IGGIE: Looks like a stage to me. And the priests look like chorus boys.

*There's a knock at the door.*

MATTHEW: Can you get that?

IGGIE: What's the password?

MATTHEW: Iggie –

IGGIE: You're the one who's ruining the wedding –

*Iggie opens the door. He sticks his head out.*

IGGIE: We're just about to come out. Well, of course I'm already out.

MATTHEW: Will you stop?

# Iggie Imagines Marriage

*Matthew runs to the trash and vomits again.*

IGGIE: No - really - we'll be out in -

*He glances at Matthew. Matthew holds up five fingers.*

IGGIE: Five minutes. I swear.

*Iggie closes the door.*

IGGIE: I'm swearing to a priest. Good thing he's your brother or he might condemn me to Hell.

*Beat.*

MATTHEW: My mother nearly had a heart attack when I asked you to be my best man.

IGGIE: I don't blame her. Any self respecting Catholic widow should have palpitations when her son decides his best man is a Jewish (by birth) atheist (by choice) nationally famous Gay (with a capital G) journalist. Of course there's the part about marrying a black woman, so her heart was weak to begin with. Why did you ask me anyway? Is it because gay men have the best taste and you needed my help to make this a true event?

MATTHEW: You're my best man, not my wedding coordinator.

IGGIE: Good point. So why'd you ask?

MATTHEW: You're my best friend.

IGGIE: Oh that.

MATTHEW: So please - no gay jokes or priest jokes -

IGGIE: How about -

MATTHEW: Or gay priest jokes. Why are you scratching?

IGGIE: I itch.

MATTHEW: You shouldn't itch. You're not getting married.

IGGIE: And so far, neither are you. Besides, I was up half the night – writing my column – which was due yesterday.

MATTHEW: You missed a deadline?

IGGIE: – and then I accidentally washed one of my contact lenses down the sink so I have to wear these ridiculous glasses. I want this day to go well for you. Hence the nerves.

MATTHEW: The glasses are cute.

IGGIE: They make me look like Sponge Bob.

MATTHEW: I always liked Sponge Bob.

IGGIE: Then why don't you marry him?

MATTHEW: You're stuck in third grade.

IGGIE: Which brother was that again?

MATTHEW: John.

*Matthew looks like he may vomit again.*

IGGIE: Right. Mark is the plumber and Luke's the cop. John – he's hot!

MATTHEW: Will you please – we're in church –

*Matthew reaches for his iPod. Iggie snatches it away.*

IGGIE: No more sports – you have to be ready to get married in five minutes! Five! You hear me young man?

MATTHEW: I know.

IGGIE: Matty, relax. Nzinga is wonderful. I'd even be interested in her – if I was "that way".

MATTHEW: She's great. I know. I just – can't imagine marriage. I don't know what it means.

IGGIE: You've discussed this with the wife to be?

# Iggie Imagines Marriage

MATTHEW: She has a hard time imagining it too.

IGGIE: Then - you're marrying the right person! So what's the problem?

MATTHEW: I hope marriage doesn't mean what it meant to my parents. Ignoring each other - except during arguments.

IGGIE: Did we have the same parents?

MATTHEW: How many minutes?

IGGIE: Three. (beat) Deep breaths.

*Matthew takes a few deep breaths.*

IGGIE: Hm.

MATTHEW: What?

IGGIE: I used to play this game - back when I was little. I would become this superhero - when I was bored -

MATTHEW: You? Bored?

IGGIE: Or when I was nervous or something. I'd become:

MATTHEW: Wonder Woman?

IGGIE: That came later.

MATTHEW: Forgive me.

IGGIE: Say ten Hail Marys. I'd become: Tim Time Traveler!

MATTHEW: How butch!

IGGIE: You know it! As Tim I could stop time -

*He does a gesture a la The Supremes.*

# Iggie Imagines Marriage

IGGIE: just stop it - at will. That way I could stop fires, capture criminals, rescue hunks in distress - all by going back in time and preventing disasters before they started.

MATTHEW: Neat.

IGGIE: "Neat"? How did you ever convince a black woman to marry you?

MATTHEW: Not sure. What made you think of that time traveler guy?

IGGIE: Tim. You asked me the time I guess. Tim would look at his watch, make note of the current time, close his eyes. Concentrate - take a few deep breaths -

*Iggie does this.*

IGGIE: and time would stop.

MATTHEW: Just like that.

IGGIE: Yeah. I was also really cute as Tim. There were days when I'd stop time, and Tim and I would - (beat) Never mind. He was the first character I wrote about when I was in my short story phase. Everything was so - solvable for him. No problems. No panic. Like you.

MATTHEW: You mean like Jefferson McCabe.

IGGIE: Yeah. He's you - sorta.

MATTHEW: I wish I was like him. But nobody's that cool and collected - least of all a subway transit cop. People love him though. That's why the show's so popular.

IGGIE: You are why the show's so popular.

MATTHEW: How many minutes?

IGGIE: Three - my watch stopped. What time do you have?

*Matthew looks at his watch.*

MATTHEW: My watch stopped too.

36

# Iggie Imagines Marriage

IGGIE: Well, it must be time. You ready?

MATTHEW: I guess.

*Iggie tries the door. It doesn't open.*

IGGIE: Does this door lock?

MATTHEW: Don't think so –

*Iggie moves aside. Matthew tries the door. It won't open.*

MATTHEW: Of all the crazy –

*He knocks on the door softly at first, then harder. Nothing happens.*

MATTHEW: Don't tell me they can't hear that –

*He pounds some more. Iggie starts scratching.*

MATTHEW: John? John!?

*Iggie glances out the window.*

IGGIE: Matt – All those people who aren't wearing hats –

MATTHEW: Yeah?

IGGIE: They're not moving either.

*Matthew turns to Iggie. He starts to smile but realizes Iggie isn't joking. He crosses to the window. Iggie starts scratching.*

MATTHEW: What's going on? Ig?

IGGIE: Well I'm not sure – exactly. Either a new kind of bomb has been dropped – or Tim Time Traveler is alive and well.

MATTHEW: That's really funny. (beat) It's not possible – is it?

*Matthew crosses to the door and pounds some more. He stops and turns to Iggie.*

# Iggie Imagines Marriage

MATTHEW: What the fuck?

IGGIE: Watch the language. We're in church.

MATTHEW: Time stopped. Time. Is that what you're telling me?

IGGIE: It's a theory.

MATTHEW: A theory? Maybe in an episode of "Black Mirror".

IGGIE: Then you explain it.

*Matthew muses over this for several moments.*

MATTHEW: You did this?

IGGIE: I – I don't know. This has never happened before. It might not have been me.

MATTHEW: Then we both died at the same time? Any minute they'll take us away to Heaven?

IGGIE: I – I don't know.

MATTHEW: Well – what did you do? If you – somehow – actually stopped time – unstop it. Now!

IGGIE: All right. I'll try – just stop looking at me like I cancelled your series.

*Iggie scratches.*

MATTHEW: Ig.

IGGIE: I'm trying to remember what I did. Oh yeah.

*Iggie looks down at his watch. He closes his eyes and breathes deeply. He opens his eyes again.*

IGGIE: Did the people start moving again?

MATTHEW: No.

# Iggie Imagines Marriage

IGGIE: That was it. That's what I did before –

MATTHEW: Do it again.

> *Iggie shakes out. He looks at his watch. He closes his eyes and breathes deeply. He opens his eyes.*

MATTHEW: Nothing.

> *Beat.*

IGGIE: We could play charades –

MATTHEW: We're stuck in the fucking Twilight Zone and you want to play charades? The least you could do is take this seriously.

> *Iggie starts scratching.*

IGGIE: I am. I'm a serious charades player! And who says this is my fault? I can't figure out how to change it back, so maybe I didn't do it to begin with.

MATTHEW: Then how did it happen?

IGGIE: You think I've stopped time before?

> *Beat.*

MATTHEW: You said you thought about it. You said Tim did it.

IGGIE: I made Tim up.

> *Beat.*

MATTHEW: Maybe it's not your fault.

IGGIE: Thank you!

MATTHEW: Since the series started I haven't been going to church as regularly. I stopped giving money to St. Martha's – I haven't been to confession in years –

IGGIE: Hold on – you think this may be a punishment – from "God"?

# Iggie Imagines Marriage

MATTHEW: My mother insists that my father would be turning in his grave if he knew that I'm marrying outside the faith -

IGGIE: Not to mention the skin tone.

MATTHEW: I've got you as my best man -

IGGIE: You actually think God cares that your best man is queer?

MATTHEW: Of course not. I don't know. I don't know what God really cares about -

IGGIE: Your mother didn't tell you?

MATTHEW: My mother is not the point.

IGGIE: Oh yes she is -

MATTHEW: Ig -

IGGIE: If she spent half as much time talking to you as she does praying for you -

MATTHEW: I'm trying to figure out what I did wrong.

IGGIE: Nothing. You're the most upstanding person I know. Except now - when you're sitting down. This time stopping has nothing to do with you - or your relationship with "God". It's so much better when you don't believe in him.

> *Iggie is still scratching.*

MATTHEW: What happens if we never figure out how to get back?

IGGIE: That won't happen.

MATTHEW: How do you know?

> *Iggie shrugs.*

MATTHEW: I've got better things to do for eternity than spending time with you.

# Iggie Imagines Marriage

IGGIE: You think I want to be stuck here with you? (beat) Wait - Tim - solved problems this way.

MATTHEW: Yeah?

IGGIE: Well, maybe there's a problem here that we - need to solve. Maybe until we solve it we'll be stuck here.

MATTHEW: What would it be?

IGGIE: Let's start with the obvious. You, my friend, are resisting this marriage thing.

MATTHEW: So -

IGGIE: So - solve it!

MATTHEW: This isn't a game show, this is my life.

IGGIE: What's the problem?

*Awkward pause.*

MATTHEW: I - just can't imagine - marriage.

IGGIE: Because of your folks?

MATTHEW: Yeah - I guess - and because - I've been - working ever since I've known her and -

IGGIE: What?

MATTHEW: What happens if the show is cancelled?

IGGIE: You can go back to the soap.

MATTHEW: I don't want to do that. It sucked - the hours - those stupid storylines - I don't want to talk about this.

IGGIE: You'd rather be stuck here?

MATTHEW: I don't know. I don't know what our life would be like if I wasn't successful. It's not the money. This career is who I am. You remember what I was like back when I was waiting tables?

IGGIE: Oh god, you were a mess.

MATTHEW: I was. And if she saw me like that – she wouldn't like it. I didn't like it. I have this feeling that that – disgruntled person – is who I really am.

IGGIE: Well – Nzinga loves you – not your career.

MATTHEW: She hasn't seen that other me: that unhappy – driven. I feel like she's getting me when I'm at my best – at the top of my career – the most – stable. What happens when I crash?

IGGIE: Who says you'll crash?

MATTHEW: It's inevitable. (beat) Being married is the last thing on my list.

IGGIE: What list?

MATTHEW: My list of things to accomplish. I don't know what you do after the last goal. God never lets you have it all. I'm overdue for a crash.

IGGIE: I haven't seen you like this since your Biology final. This is not a reason to call off a wedding. You're not going to crash.

MATTHEW: I – just want to deserve her. I'm not sure I do.

IGGIE: She loves you – and you have a great time together. You deserve that.

*Beat.*

MATTHEW: You ever feel this way? This nervous about the future – about anyone?

*Iggie scratches.*

IGGIE: Have we solved your problem?

# Iggie Imagines Marriage

MATTHEW: We can't be here to solve my problem. It's not solvable. And if it was – wouldn't I be stuck here with a – therapist or something?

IGGIE: I've had lots of therapy.

> *Beat. Iggie stands, looks out the window, then runs toward the door, hitting it with his shoulder. It doesn't move.*

MATTHEW: What are you doing?

IGGIE: Realizing I'm not Wonder Woman.

MATTHEW: Ig – what's wrong?

IGGIE: If the problem is not yours to solve maybe it's mine to solve. And I'm such a fucking mess that by the time we discover which problem of mine needs solving we may both be ready for a nursing home.

MATTHEW: It can't be that bad. Whatever it is, I'll help you.

> *Iggie puts his face in his hands.*

IGGIE: Shit. My nose is bleeding again.

> *Matthew grabs him a tissue. Iggie removes his glasses and holds his head back.*

MATTHEW: Pinch tightly.

IGGIE: Thanks nosebleed coach.

MATTHEW: I'm trying to help. (beat) I thought you wanted to get out of here.

IGGIE: I've changed my mind.

MATTHEW: I'm gonna be stuck here indefinitely because you don't want to talk.

IGGIE: What? I'm supposed to launch into a discussion of my problems just like that?

43

MATTHEW: I had to.

IGGIE: And a lot of good it did us.

MATTHEW: Come on – let's deal with it – so we can get out of here. I don't want to be stuck here because you're too stubborn to open your fucking mouth about whatever the hell is bothering you – it's not fair.

IGGIE: You think it's fair that I've been spending my whole afternoon holding your hand and telling you to get married?

*Matthew grabs Iggie's hand.*

MATTHEW: Thank you for holding my hand all afternoon. Now I'm returning the favor.

*Iggie scratches.*

MATTHEW: What?

*Beat.*

IGGIE: I don't want you to get married.

MATTHEW: How come?

IGGIE: You gotta promise not to hate me.

MATTHEW: I won't.

IGGIE: You won't promise or you won't hate me?

MATTHEW: I won't hate you.

IGGIE: I love you.

MATTHEW: I love you too.

IGGIE: No – I'm in love with you.

*Beat.*

MATTHEW: Oh. Of course –

# Iggie Imagines Marriage

IGGIE: What the hell does that mean?

MATTHEW: I knew that.

IGGIE: Bullshit. How?

MATTHEW: I don't know - I know you - so I guess I know how you feel about me. The way you look at me sometimes - like - like you just won the Pulitzer. And that summer we lived together - all that sunning by the pool - I get certain vibes from you.

IGGIE: Why didn't you say something?

MATTHEW: What would I say? It's all right.

IGGIE: It's not all right. I've been - planning - plotting - premeditating - ways to stop this wedding.

MATTHEW: Like how?

IGGIE: I thought of leaving the ring at home. I thought of being late and making all of you wait for me. I thought of being early and setting the church on fire. Why am I telling you this?

MATTHEW: I asked.

IGGIE: That's why I was up half the night. It had nothing to do with an article for the magazine. It had everything to do with you.

*Beat.*

MATTHEW: How were you going to set the church on fire?

IGGIE: Stop making fun of me!

MATTHEW: So, you're in love with me. Big deal. (beat) You remember Jennifer Smith - from college? Sarah Pettaway? Andy Brackton?

IGGIE: Yeah?

MATTHEW: They were all in love with me too.

# Iggie Imagines Marriage

IGGIE: You arrogant bastard.

MATTHEW: I'm not. I've looked like this - all my life. I have great metabolism. I never had acne, or a single cavity - I've never had - corns - or bad breath or anything. I don't know why.

IGGIE: You're perfect, that's why.

MATTHEW: I was taught to be open and honest and friendly. And people are drawn to me. It's always been there. Like the way I've always liked rich desserts, and how I hate for my feet to be cold. It's part of who I am.

IGGIE: I'm so embarrassed - I can't be in love with you.

MATTHEW: I don't care!

IGGIE: I've spent my whole life trying to capitalize on how - unique I am. I finally get the courage to tell you that I'm in love with you and you say "Yeah. Everybody is - join the club." You wound me!

MATTHEW: If I had to stop being friends with everyone I'd ever suspected had feelings for me I'd - I don't know what I'd do. I'd only talk to - accountants - and eunuchs and - clergy. I care about you. I just - don't care that you have feelings for me.

IGGIE: I talk to you sometimes when you're not around. I wear things I know you like. I want to be with you all the time. And I'm annoyed at myself because for someone as out as me to be so fixated on someone as straight as you - it's just not - P.C. (beat) I don't want Nzinga to marry you - I want to marry you. Why are you still holding my hand?

MATTHEW: I don't care.

IGGIE: You're a terrible tease.

MATTHEW: By the way it's "I". "For someone as out as I" you said me. You know - "as out as I am" - the am is understood.

IGGIE: Even when you're annoying - you're so cute!

*Beat.*

# Iggie Imagines Marriage

IGGIE: You're not - by any chance - in love with me too?

MATTHEW: No.

IGGIE: It's O.K. I don't care. Well of course I do care - but - I mean I knew you weren't - in love with me - but - you know - I was hoping against hope that I might - get a kiss or something.

MATTHEW: Come on!

IGGIE: You gotta ask.

MATTHEW: No you don't!

IGGIE: Maybe we're in this - time warp to - actually get together. Maybe that's God's plan -

MATTHEW: You don't believe in God.

IGGIE: If I got you I might. I'm sorry. That sounds really horrible - and I - value you too much as a friend to mess that up. I think. But I also think that if we were to - fool around -

MATTHEW: What?

IGGIE: No one would know but us -

MATTHEW: God would know. I would know! I can't believe you'd be that selfish.

IGGIE: It's not like you're married yet.

MATTHEW: I would be by now -

IGGIE: Don't you blame this on me - you're here too.

MATTHEW: So?

IGGIE: We needed to discuss this - both of us. How do I really know you're not also - maybe - kinda attracted to me too?

MATTHEW: I told you -

# Iggie Imagines Marriage

IGGIE: You're lying. Are you trying to say that never ever were you attracted to me – not once? Is that what you're saying?

MATTHEW: Look – you're attractive. Objectively –

IGGIE: And –

MATTHEW: and – when you came out to me I can't say that I didn't think about – in a general way – what it might be like to – think of men – sexually.

IGGIE: Me?

MATTHEW: Among other men – yes – I thought of you – yes – in an – objective kind of way.

IGGIE: You tried me out. (beat) How was I?

MATTHEW: You're really enjoying this.

IGGIE: You thought of me – you tried me out – objectively. You know what that means?

MATTHEW: Nothing. What?

IGGIE: It means – that – maybe we – do – belong together.

MATTHEW: No.

IGGIE: I always thought we did. And – you thought about it. Well –

MATTHEW: Well, what?

*Iggie kneels.*

IGGIE: Well – Marry me.

MATTHEW: No.

IGGIE: I wish I could make you marry me – but I know that if something – sublime happened here – I'd want more – I'd want all of you. You're so great.

# Iggie Imagines Marriage

MATTHEW: I'm not great.

IGGIE: No, you are. See, you don't even know. This is a bona fide first class tragedy that you don't know how wonderful you are - how spectacular we could be. Fabulous - fantastic - marvelous - mythic - mellifluous. (beat) Kiss me.

MATTHEW: No!

IGGIE: Think of it as the ultimate test. You thought of me - objectively - God knows I thought of you. Here we are - stuck. You're afraid there'll be fireworks.

MATTHEW: That's not it.

IGGIE: Then pucker up.

MATTHEW: No!

IGGIE: If you're so sure.

MATTHEW: I am sure.

IGGIE: Are you? When we lived together - I used to pretend - we were together. It was a whole - pathetic Carol Brady thing. I'd make dinner for two and then I'd sit there and imagine that you'd walk in and I'd ask you about your day and hand you your slippers.

MATTHEW: I didn't wear slippers.

IGGIE: I bought you some.

MATTHEW: With plaid insoles.

IGGIE: With plaid insoles.

MATTHEW: Right: brown corduroy.

IGGIE: You loved them.

MATTHEW: I did.

IGGIE: And the dinners.

# Iggie Imagines Marriage

MATTHEW: You're a good cook.

IGGIE: When I'm cooking for you.

MATTHEW: And after we'd play Scrabble and you would pull out these words no one had ever heard of. Like "hypertrophy" with that look of triumph on your face. And you'd define it.

IGGIE: "A non-tumorous enlargement of an organ or tissue."

MATTHEW: Like that. Best Summer of my life. (beat) I want to go back.

IGGIE: To that house?

MATTHEW: To my wedding.

IGGIE: We're not finished yet.

MATTHEW: We are. If I have to be completely ready before we can go - I am - now completely ready. Let's do it.

IGGIE: Do what?

MATTHEW: Stop!

IGGIE: One kiss - one peck - and we'll know once and for all if we were meant to be - together. And if not - we'll know that too. You can get on with your wedding and I can retire my fantasy if that's the way it turns out. No one has to know.

> *Beat.*

MATTHEW: All right.

IGGIE: Really?

MATTHEW: Just to shut you up. Come on.

> *Iggie stands.*

IGGIE: Oh my god. You're so cute! How long I've waited for this -

# Iggie Imagines Marriage

MATTHEW: Cut the 'celebrating diva' routine –

IGGIE: That was my 'romantic heroine'.

MATTHEW: Just kiss me –

> *Matthew sits and closes his eyes. Iggie sidles up to him. He wriggles a bit excitedly. (beat) Matthew opens his eyes.*

MATTHEW: Ig!

> *Matthew grabs him and kisses him. They remain lip locked for a moment. They pull apart. Iggie sits. Long beat.*

MATTHEW: You feel that?

IGGIE: What?

MATTHEW: Nothing. Not a thing.

> *Beat.*

IGGIE: Yeah.

MATTHEW: Zilch – zero – zip –

IGGIE: You're not even a good kisser. You – Mr. Perfect. That was really lame – lethargic. You were holding back.

MATTHEW: Holding back what?

IGGIE: You could have used a little tongue.

MATTHEW: There was – nothing there.

IGGIE: Not even a spark.

MATTHEW: That's a relief.

IGGIE: For you maybe –

MATTHEW: For both of us. Now we know. This wedding is the right thing. I'm ready to go.

# Iggie Imagines Marriage

IGGIE: I feel cheated.

MATTHEW: What now? You need more proof - a blowjob and you'll be all set?

IGGIE: Prick. This is a big deal for me. Let me mourn you - just a little bit. That was a major disappointment. Where do you learn to (Makes a smooching gesture.) like that?

MATTHEW: I'm not going to sit here while you insult me. I'm supposed to be getting married.

IGGIE: Blame me - when I've been such a great sport helping you plan your big heterosexual union fest.

MATTHEW: You didn't have to.

IGGIE: I'd rather be with you than cruising Today's Man. Men? At least I thought I would until I kissed you. I'm sorry.

MATTHEW: Let's go back. I listened to you - I kissed you even. Now I'm not gonna be kept hostage by you - demanding or insisting that I need to do more before we can get time moving again. (beat) You do realize that even if I was "that way" I couldn't actually be in a relationship with you.

IGGIE: Why?

MATTHEW: We'd have to talk about everything so - intensely.

IGGIE: We already do that - what would be the difference?

MATTHEW: I might have to kill you. (beat) Ready?

IGGIE: Ready.

> *Iggie takes a glance at his watch. Matthew glances at his watch for good measure. They both close their eyes and take three deep breaths. They open their eyes.*

MATTHEW: Did it work?

> *Matthew goes to the window.*

# Iggie Imagines Marriage

MATTHEW: The people aren't moving. Shit.

IGGIE: You are ready to get married now aren't you? Matt?

MATTHEW: I'm ready. I just –

IGGIE: What –

MATTHEW: enjoyed that moment with you – and wanted it to last a little longer. Let's not make a huge deal out of it –

IGGIE: If I could time travel on a regular basis I'd be so busy going back in time to revisit my favorite moments I wouldn't get to create any new ones.

MATTHEW: I'm ready.

IGGIE: You sure?

MATTHEW: Yes.

> *They look at their watches and close their eyes. They take three deep breaths. Outside the snow starts. They open their eyes. Iggie looks toward the window.*

IGGIE: It's snowing!!!!

> *They hug.*

MATTHEW: Check the door.

> *Iggie does. It opens. He looks out. Matthew looks at his watch.*

IGGIE: They haven't moved an inch.

MATTHEW: Like only a second has passed.

IGGIE: You think we can do it again?

MATTHEW: No! Are you nuts? (beat) How do I look?

IGGIE: Stunning.

*Matthew takes a deep breath.*

MATTHEW: Got the ring?

*Iggie reaches into his pocket. He fishes around.*

IGGIE: Uh –

MATTHEW: What uh? God – please Ig –

IGGIE: I can run home – it won't take –

MATTHEW: God – dear God.

*Matthew grabs his stomach, he kneels down by the waste basket. Iggie produces the ring.*

IGGIE: Oh – look.

MATTHEW: Bitch.

IGGIE: Ms. Bitch to you.

MATTHEW: Let's go.

*Iggie holds his arm out. Matthew links arms with him. They exit. Wedding bells ring.*

*Blackout.*

# UNDERSTANDING

*"Do the best you can until you know better,*
*then when you can, do better."*

*-Maya Angelou*

# Like the End of the World

# Like the End of the World

*There's a phone ringing. Lights up on Kendrick, late 30s, black - he wears a military uniform. Ryan, white, and around his age, is standing next to him. He wears a suit and is covered with white/gray dust.*

KENDRICK: Why isn't she answering?

RYAN: She's coming.

KENDRICK: She could be asleep.

RYAN: She's not.

*Lights up on Shelly, black 30s.*

SHELLY: Hello.

RYAN: See –

KENDRICK: What took you so long?

SHELLY: It was only a few rings. (beat) I'm glad you called.

KENDRICK: Doesn't sound like you. Is there static?

SHELLY: Not that I'm hearing.

KENDRICK: How's Mom?

SHELLY: She's – fine.

KENDRICK: Well what happened?

SHELLY: To Mom? Nothing.

KENDRICK: Then what happened to you?

SHELLY: What do you mean?

KENDRICK: You said it was urgent – that I call. So I'm calling. I only have a few minutes, Shell.

SHELLY: Ok. (beat) You should come home.

RYAN: You should.

KENDRICK: I'm not going through this again.

SHELLY: Mom's worried about you. She still can't believe you went. It's not the right thing.

KENDRICK: It is the right thing.

SHELLY: Nobody else thinks it is.

KENDRICK: There are a lot of soldiers here, Shelly. You want to talk to them? To us it's the right thing.

SHELLY: Ryan wouldn't think so.

RYAN: Huh.

KENDRICK: Ryan's not here.

SHELLY: That doesn't mean you don't think about him. He wouldn't want you over there.

RYAN: She's right about that.

KENDRICK: He doesn't get to choose. I'm not doing this tonight. You said it was urgent.

SHELLY: It is.

KENDRICK: (To Ryan.) Did you talk to her?

RYAN: That's your job.

SHELLY: What?

KENDRICK: What?

SHELLY: I didn't hear what you said.

KENDRICK: I was talking to myself.

*Beat.*

SHELLY: You kill anybody yet?

KENDRICK: Shelly –

SHELLY: Have you?

KENDRICK: No.

SHELLY: Will you tell me if you do?

KENDRICK: I – There's so much about being here that you don't know – that you can't understand.

SHELLY: I don't want to understand. I just – we just want you home. This is not going to solve anything. You don't believe in this.

KENDRICK: I do – I have to do something.

SHELLY: This isn't it.

RYAN: Listen to her.

KENDRICK: I gotta go.

SHELLY: I'm – dating.

*Beat.*

KENDRICK: Ok.

RYAN: She's what?

SHELLY: That's what I wanted to tell you.

KENDRICK: Ok.

SHELLY: He's really nice. And – uh – I met him at school.

KENDRICK: Why did you want to tell me this?

SHELLY: Because – I thought you'd want to know.

KENDRICK: Ok. Uh – am I supposed to – guess why you'd think I'd want to know – all the way over here – that you're dating somebody all the way over there?

SHELLY: He's Muslim.

*Beat.*

KENDRICK: You don't know any Muslims. (beat) Is this for real?

*Ryan shrugs.*

SHELLY: Yusef. He's really fun. He likes model trains.

KENDRICK: Does he blow them up?

RYAN: Oh, god!

SHELLY: That's completely ignorant and stupid.

KENDRICK: So is this phone call.

SHELLY: It's not.

RYAN: Tell her.

KENDRICK: Shelly –

SHELLY: His family is from Iraq.

KENDRICK: I'm sorry?

SHELLY: They're Americans, but they have people there.

KENDRICK: Why are you telling me this?

SHELLY: It's – my news.

KENDRICK: Shelly – Are you – You're not dating this guy – because I'm here. Are you?

SHELLY: Everything's not about you, Kendrick.

RYAN: Hah!

KENDRICK: Shut up.

SHELLY: What?

KENDRICK: Some guy here. (beat) You said this was urgent. That you needed to talk to me. About this?

SHELLY: Yes.

RYAN: She just doesn't know how to get through to you.

KENDRICK: Are you dating him because I'm going to Baghdad?

SHELLY: You won't come home.

KENDRICK: How is that an answer to my –

SHELLY: It's – you said you didn't know what to do – when Ryan died.

RYAN: You still don't.

SHELLY: And you made your choice to go there –

RYAN: A bad choice. Tell her –

SHELLY: And Mom and I – I can't speak for her – except that she's not sleeping – much – well she is now because she's on Tylenol PM – but if she weren't medicated she wouldn't be.

KENDRICK: This is ridiculous –

SHELLY: It's not. I didn't know what to do either. I didn't know. I mean the whole thing that happened to Ryan was –

RYAN: Surreal.

SHELLY: I know you loved him. I loved him too. And I didn't know what to do – so –

KENDRICK: So you're dating this –

SHELLY: Yes. It's – a family karma thing. I don't see why you don't see that. You're over there – doing whatever –

KENDRICK: Helping.

RYAN: Tell her!

SHELLY: Doing your – military – negative thing – and I'm – balancing it out.

KENDRICK: Are you still in therapy?

SHELLY: I just wanted you to know. As long as you're doing – that – I'll be – doing this. I like Yusef. He's sweet. And he's taught me all about Ramadan –

KENDRICK: Good lord.

SHELLY: On our dates – we talk. We don't eat much. Because he's fasting all the time. Not all the time, but you know.

RYAN: If you went home –

KENDRICK: I'm not leaving.

RYAN: Then say goodbye. (beat) Then tell her you know you're not going to see her again. Tell her you know for sure.

SHELLY: Are you there?

KENDRICK: Yeah. (beat) He treats you nice?

SHELLY: He does.

KENDRICK: What's his last name?

SHELLY: So you can call him up or something? (beat) I'm not telling you.

RYAN: So you want this. Is that it? Your big plan?

KENDRICK: You're an ass.

SHELLY: I'm an ass?

KENDRICK: No, I'm sorry, Shell – Not you. It's – privacy's almost impossible here. There's always someone digging at you.

SHELLY: Tell 'em to leave you alone. (beat) I miss you. You can come home.

RYAN: Go.

KENDRICK: I can't. We know what we're doing here.

RYAN: Yeah. I guess you do.

*Beat.*

SHELLY: So you're not coming –

KENDRICK: I'm not.

RYAN: Coming to see me.

*Beat.*

SHELLY: I think about Ryan all the time. You ever think about how he was at the end? If he was brave?

RYAN: Yes. Tell her yes.

SHELLY: Did he know he wasn't going to make it out? Sense it was going to be – over – like the end of the world. I dream about it sometimes. Do you? (beat) In my dream he runs – down the steps.

RYAN: But you can't outrun it.

SHELLY: And all at once: a roar as everything collapses.

KENDRICK: Shelly –

SHELLY: The floor beneath his feet. The walls. What?

# Like the End of the World

KENDRICK: I'd rather not hear about it.

SHELLY: There's got to have been a moment when he knew. Where it was what it was.

*Beat.*

KENDRICK: What if it doesn't work out with Yusef? I don't want you getting hurt.

SHELLY: You should be getting a care package in a few days. Socks. Cookies. That peanut butter you like.

KENDRICK: What kind of cookies?

SHELLY: Cashew chocolate chip.

*Beat.*

KENDRICK: Tell Mom, I said hi. And that I love her.

SHELLY: Yeah. I will.

RYAN: Maybe I don't want you like this. I won't talk to you when you show up.

KENDRICK: I do think about Ryan all the time. I pray for him and his family.

SHELLY: Good. Yeah.

KENDRICK: Look - Shelly -

SHELLY: What?

KENDRICK: - if anything happens to me. You know where the papers are -

SHELLY: Yeah, I do.

*Beat.*

KENDRICK: Ok, I should go. (beat) Other guys want to use the phone. Say hi to Mom. (beat) I love you. So much.

SHELLY: Yeah. Me too. Be careful.

KENDRICK: I will.

*Kendrick hangs up.*

RYAN: You could have told her.

KENDRICK: What's the point?

RYAN: She'd have some warning. No one ever gets that.

KENDRICK: Except me.

RYAN: Even if she didn't believe you –

KENDRICK: You said it – I can't outrun it. I don't intend to. And I can't wait to hold you.

*Kendrick and Ryan stare at each other.*

*Blackout.*

# Three People

# Three People

*A video chat. Each person will be seen in their own space. A CHIME as lights come up on two rooms.*

*We're in a cozy bedroom. It's nighttime. Nia, 30s, black, upscale and cheerful is getting set up on her computer. She's settling into a seated position on her bed wearing a T-shirt and sweatpants.*

*We're also in a kitchen. Well decorated and upscale. Reed, 30s, black, his exhaustion poking through his normal polish. He's impatient as Nia gets settled.*

REED: Hey. Can you hear me?

*She's still getting settled.*

REED: Nia?

NIA: Hi. Did you just get home?

REED: Pretty much.

NIA: How was it?

REED: Like yesterday. Like the day before.

NIA: It's not getting better? That's what the news says. That people are healing – or whatever. Less sick people.

REED: Fewer.

NIA: Whatever. Isn't it better?

REED: It's a hospital. So the people who come in –

NIA: – are sick, right. You look tired.

REED: Thanks.

NIA: I'm being honest with you. What's up?

REED: Did you go out today?

# Three People

NIA: Why?

REED: That march went right past your place.

NIA: Not right past.

REED: Your neighborhood. Did you go?

NIA: Why would I go?

REED: You're not answering the question, Nia.

NIA: I don't like when you're like this.

REED: I heard you were out there.

NIA: From who? Whom?

REED: Carlo. He said he saw you.

NIA: Since when do you listen to him?

REED: Since I'm concerned about you.

NIA: Haven't seen him in forever. He's not reliable. Proven that over and over again. Creep. Where did you see him?

REED: Doesn't matter - if you weren't there. I know you were upset about the murder.

NIA: You were, too. You told me you were crying.

REED: I got teary is what I said. I didn't go march. I wouldn't be that reckless.

NIA: You're bringing this up because of fucking Carlo?

REED: Why would he lie? You said you couldn't sleep - that you couldn't hear any more about it on the news.

NIA: Doesn't mean I was in the street.

REED: So you stayed home?

NIA: I can take care of myself, Reed. I'm not twelve. I don't need rescuing. I don't need you thinking you have to -

REED: Fine. If you weren't out there. You haven't exactly said.

NIA: Carlo's a liar.

REED: And you didn't march.

NIA: No.

REED: Ok. (beat) People are still dying from this thing -

NIA: What happened? Did you lose someone?

REED: I don't want to talk about it. (beat) Yes, it's - Just, please don't go outside. With your asthma - Maybe when I come over. We can go for a walk or something.

NIA: I take walks. Not near people.

REED: I'd rather you didn't.

NIA: You're paranoid.

REED: I'm still right.

NIA: You've got 'rescuer' burned on your forehead.

REED: Do not.

NIA: The time you carried me to the hospital -

REED: That was scary. I saved your life.

NIA: 20 years ago.

REED: Still counts.

> They laugh.

REED: Could you hear it? Were they loud?

NIA: It sounded amazing. They were chanting: "I Can't Breathe!" "No justice, no peace."

REED: Dad would have been out there. Raising his fist.

NIA: Yelling his head off. Using that bullhorn.

*Laughter. Awkward silence.*

REED: You do anything today – around Dad?

NIA: Not really.

REED: You always do something.

NIA: Not always.

REED: Yeah, always.

*Beat.*

NIA: Ok. I went out there.

REED: Nia –

NIA: I couldn't sit in here anymore. Sick and tired of watching it on the news. Seeing Facebook posts. Getting texts from white friends telling me they love me. That they care so much. If that's so fucking true why can't they stop the police from killing us? So I went. Stepped out there and felt it. The street crackling with revolution. I was punching the air and channeling Dad. And he was with me.

REED: How close did you get?

NIA: I don't know. I don't remember. I know it felt good.

REED: That's fucking reckless.

NIA: I don't get to do anything reckless anymore. I barely get to do anything.

REED: You have work!

NIA: I'm tired of my work. Tired of everything.

REED: I'm tired of seeing black people dying.

NIA: Me, too.

REED: I don't want you to be among them. What would be the point of that?

*Beat.*

NIA: I'm glad I went.

REED: Let the white people be out there.

NIA: Tell that to Jessica.

REED: She knows how I feel.

NIA: It's our fight.

REED: We're losing.

NIA: Not today. Today I was out there in it. Today I won.

REED: Please, Nia. Don't do it again. Promise me.

NIA: No. (beat) Too much is at stake.

REED: I know. (beat) Three people.

NIA: What?

REED: I saw three people die today.

NIA: I'm sorry.

*Beat.*

REED: I should get some rest.

NIA: Ok. Thanks for – reaching out. I guess.

REED: You guess?

*She considers this.*

NIA: Love you.

REED: I love you.

*He waves. A CHIME is heard.*

*Blackout.*

# Actual Cost

*Manhattan. Saturday. An almost empty subway car. Iyana, black, and B.T., white, both late 20s, sit next to each other, his arm is around her. Both are dressed nicely in business attire. She looks incredible. He looks uncomfortable in these clothes. He stares at her for a beat.*

B.T.: We should go back.

IYANA: I'm not going to be late. (beat) Honey, did you brush?

B.T.: Yes.

*Beat. Annoyed, he pulls out gum. Pops it in his mouth. Chews.*

B.T.: Nobody will notice if we're late. It's a big church.

IYANA: Aunt Gwenny will notice.

B.T.: I'm getting off at the next stop.

IYANA: No. I'm not showing up alone, it's a wedding.

*Beat.*

B.T.: Then you'll have to lend me twenty dollars.

IYANA: I only have –

B.T.: How about ten?

IYANA: You always –

B.T.: 'yana –

IYANA: Why do you need it? (beat) So you can buy some cigarettes?

B.T.: I quit. You know I quit.

*She smiles.*

IYANA: You did, didn't you? (beat) One bad habit down. You'll live longer.

B.T.: Longer for you. With you.

*Beat.*

IYANA: What do you want it for?

B.T.: I have to justify it, like I'm 10? God, 'yana - if I hadn't forgotten my wallet -

IYANA: But you did. Too busy watching ESPN. You're always -

B.T.: Not always -

IYANA: addicted. (beat) I'm already paying for your train ride. How much do you owe me?

B.T.: Don't make it about that -

IYANA: What do you want it for? (beat) The lottery? (beat) The lottery's -

IYANA: a scam.

B.T.: an opportunity - It's my money.

IYANA: If you pay me back.

> *Michael enters the car. He's black, and clearly effeminate. His clothes look dirty and he's not wearing shoes. They look up at him for a moment and then look away. Michael smiles and slowly sits on the same bench as they are - closer to B.T. Michael is watching. They notice. Beat.*

B.T.: For weddings - the lottery - marks the occasion - it's lucky. I play the date and the -

IYANA: - number of letters in the names of the -

B.T.: - bride and groom. A sweet and important gesture. (beat) If it'll make you feel better, you won't get any when I win. Your conscience will be clear. I'll buy a mansion, you'll get the basement - the broom closet. (beat) Fine. I'll ask Greg. He'll spot me.

IYANA: Before or after he says his vows?

*Beat. They laugh.*

MICHAEL: How y'all doing?

*B.T. nods.*

MICHAEL: Always about money, isn't it?

*He laughs. B.T. joins in.*

IYANA: Not always.

MICHAEL: Much of the time, honey.

> *The train slows down and stops. The lights dim and come back. On the loudspeaker an announcement:*

CONDUCTOR: Ladies and gentlemen, [static] train up ahead of us, we should be [static] shortly.

> *Iyana looks at her watch. Beat.*

MICHAEL: Haven't eaten in two days. Trying to get me enough to get something to eat –

> *Awkward pause.*

B.T.: Sorry, man.

MICHAEL: Don't be sorry. Be generous.

B.T.: Left my wallet at home. That's – we were – discussing.

> *Michael looks at him.*

B.T.: Didn't I leave my wallet at home?

IYANA: He left it at home.

> *B.T. shrugs. Beat.*

MICHAEL: Miss? Haven't I seen you around?

B.T.: No. (beat) You haven't seen her around. (beat) He hasn't seen you
- has he?

MICHAEL: You ride this train a lot?

B.T.: Everybody does.

MICHAEL: She does. I never forget a face. You ride this. Right, Miss?

IYANA: I do actually.

MICHAEL: Well, this is my train, too. So - we've seen each other. You
seen me - I've seen you.

*B.T. shifts a bit uncomfortably.*

MICHAEL: Well, hi.

IYANA: Hi.

B.T.: Hi.

CONDUCTOR: We apologize for any inconvenience. [static] moving
[static].

MICHAEL: Miss, I'm trying to get myself something –

B.T.: She doesn't have anything.

IYANA: Maybe. (beat) Maybe I do.

*Beat. Iyana pulls out her purse and reaches into it.*

B.T.: You're going to give him –

MICHAEL: Michael.

*He half waves at them.*

B.T.: You're going to give Michael –

IYANA: If I have something, yes.

MICHAEL: I do remember you. Mm hm - generous.

B.T.: You said you only had -

IYANA: I don't have any change. Sorry.

*Michael nods. B.T. relaxes.*

MICHAEL: Any bills?

B.T.: Look -

MICHAEL: I'm hungry. Beyond hungry. It's a question, okay? She can't answer an honest question? You underestimate her.

B.T.: If she doesn't have change, then she doesn't have bills.

MICHAEL: Don't let him belittle you -

*She smiles. Beat.*

MICHAEL: (To B.T.) She knows people can have bills but not change. That change isn't the only option. There are other - choices. You know? A dollar - a dollar is a dream.

B.T.: You're - it's illegal to beg for money -

IYANA: B.T. -

MICHAEL: A dollar is a prayer. You got something against prayer?

*Beat. Iyana stares at Michael for a moment. She looks at B.T. Beat. She looks in her purse.*

B.T.: Iyana - (To Michael.) She doesn't have -

IYANA: I might.

B.T.: What? Bills?

MICHAEL: What do you got against donations, sir? Tithing -

B.T.: This is not –

IYANA: I don't – I don't – no –

MICHAEL: A five is good. A five is a sandwich.

B.T.: Hey!

MICHAEL: A ten is maybe some Chinese food. A ten is ten prayers.
Ten dreams.

B.T.: Move on!

IYANA: B.T.!

MICHAEL: Hey, mister man – we're all out here – we're all the same.
We need to help each other, you and me.

B.T.: You can't help me.

MICHAEL: (To Iyana.) Why's he so negative? (To B.T.) What's the
difference between us? We out here working it – it's hard, right? But all
of us – on the train, on the planet. Next 100 people you see – that's 100
people praying.

B.T.: God.

MICHAEL: Right. To God. For better things. Something's always
coming between you and your actual life, right? Maybe I got more
somethings between me and mine. That's it – the only difference. So I
ask for help –

B.T.: It's not your money.

MICHAEL: Is it yours?

B.T.: Shut up!

IYANA: Honey – stop it.

> *B.T. stands.*

B.T.: (To Michael.) Shut the fuck up.

IYANA: Honey.

*She stands too, puts a hand on his shoulder.*

CONDUCTOR: The train ahead [static] clearing the station, we'll be [static].

IYANA: Sit down. (beat) Please.

*Beat. He looks at her – softens. She gestures that he sit on the other side of her. He shakes his head and returns to his spot next to Michael. He looks straight ahead. Beat. She crosses to the other side of Michael, crouches down beside him. They look into each other's faces. B.T. turns away in disgust.*

MICHAEL: Maybe I'm asleep, you know, sister? Snoring – right here – or in a doorway. Hoping: half a bagel – one whole dollar – ten prayers – twenty – fifty dreams – asking for whatever – hoping for whatever. People getting all unapproachable. I'm getting hungrier. Looking for a hundred – praying – for a million. One at a time if that's all I get. Anything. One at a time if that's all there is.

*She pulls a bill from her purse and presses it into his hand.*

B.T.: What are you giving him?

MICHAEL: Thank you, honey. Thanks so much.

IYANA: Good luck.

MICHAEL: God bless you, sister.

*Iyana returns to her seat. They all sit there a moment. The train begins to move. Michael stands – hovers near B.T.*

MICHAEL: You really cute, you know that.

*Michael winks. B.T. glares at him. Michael exits laughing. Beat.*

B.T.: What the hell?

IYANA: Honey, it's over.

B.T.: What did you give him?

IYANA: He was hungry. We're not hungry - he's got nothing -

B.T.: You don't know what he's got. You don't know anything about him, but how he looks - smells. Would you give him anything if he was white?

IYANA: Oh fuck you. Not everything is affirmative action.

B.T.: Fuck you.

IYANA: Why are you so caught up in me taking care of you?

B.T.: Why are you caught up in taking care of anyone but me?

IYANA: That's ridiculous.

B.T.: Your mother, Rosetta, Billy. (beat) I'm getting off at the next stop. (beat) There's all kinds of hungry 'yana. (beat) You want to feed the homeless? You hate that begging shit. But today you bend over backwards for some queer - con man. Dammit 'yana - affirmative action. That's bullshit - Anyone but me. Anyone. (beat) I'm getting my wallet.

IYANA: You're going to show up, right? You're not going to - not show up.

B.T.: I need my money, that's all.

IYANA: God. It won't be - I know you'll find something -

B.T.: Don't -

> She starts to cry, covers her face. B.T. turns to her. The train screeches to a stop.

CONDUCTOR: One hundred - twenty fifth street. Transfer for the C [static] trains.

> The sound of the door opening. B.T. stares at her, then at the door. The sound of the door closing.

CONDUCTOR: Fifty ninth street next.

*B.T. stares out. Iyana looks up, surprised he's still there.*

IYANA: Aren't you going?

B.T.: I can get it later. Won't stay at the reception. Something.

*The sound of the train moving. B.T. crosses back to sit on the other side of Iyana. They both stare out, not touching.*

*He pulls out a piece of gum. Offers it to her. She won't take it. He looks over at her, then away. She looks at him, then away. Then, slowly, not looking at each other, she takes his hand. The sound of the train fills the space.*

*Blackout.*

# POLITICS

*"Everything can be explained to people, on the single condition that you want them to understand."*

*-Frantz Fanon*

# Special Counsel

*Projected above the stage: "...Mueller is a superb choice to be special counsel." -Newt Gingrich, May 2017*

*Lights up on William, 30s, black, in a suit and tie. He's at a desk, in an office. He picks up his cell phone. Puts it down. Picks it up again. Swipes. His thumb dances on the device. He puts it down. Picks it up again. Presses a button. Somewhere else a phone rings. Lights up on a living room, Cordelia, 30s, white, enters. Grabs the phone.*

CORDELIA: Yeah?

WILLIAM: Hi. I'm looking for Mrs. Muller. Does she – Is this her place? Roberta Muller?

CORDELIA: This is her place. (beat) Who is this?

WILLIAM: I'm a – I was a student of hers: William Samuels.

CORDELIA: Oh my god. Hi! It's Cord.

WILLIAM: Oh, hey, Cord. I didn't expect to – do you live there?

CORDELIA: I don't really – but I do now, kind of. I'm back for a bit. I guess. How are you?

WILLIAM: Ok. I'm a lawyer.

CORDELIA: That's what you do, not how you are.

WILLIAM: Right. I'm fine. Busy. Married. I have a good life. Mostly. You?

CORDELIA: Ok. Mom hasn't been well –

WILLIAM: Oh no.

CORDELIA: It's ok. She's not dead. She's just old. We're all heading there. We moved her into a place. It's nice – for that kind of place. But – she lives here normally. Used to, I guess. That's kind of how I am. Figuring it out. Whatever. (beat) How are your parents?

WILLIAM: They're fine. When did you move her?

CORDELIA: Last week. It was time. (beat) Funny to talk to you. You weren't at the last reunion.

WILLIAM: I don't really want to see anybody.

CORDELIA: Thanks.

WILLIAM: I didn't mean you.

CORDELIA: You haven't been in touch.

WILLIAM: Neither have you.

> *Beat.*

CORDELIA: You called to say something to Mom?

> *Beat.*

WILLIAM: I did. (beat) I - hate my job. Corporate law is the worst. Money's good. But the rest is - I'm dying. It's time to do something else. (beat) And I've been having these dreams.

CORDELIA: About my mother?

WILLIAM: It's stupid - nothing. It's weird.

CORDELIA: It's sounding weird.

WILLIAM: I'm thinking of quitting - the job - and going into politics. I think.

CORDELIA: Really?

WILLIAM: The Senate - maybe. I might run. Against -

CORDELIA: Oh, you'd win. She's terrible. All those people are terrible. Politics.

WILLIAM: I'm not a woman and it's supposed to be the year of the woman. (beat) But with everything that's going on: the news! I can't even watch. I listen. NPR. It's ridiculous.

CORDELIA: Absurd. (beat) If you're a senator you can't turn it off.

WILLIAM: I know. (beat) I started boxing. I take lessons. I had to beat something up. I keep thinking I should do something. That I should be in there. Fighting.

CORDELIA: I'm not brave enough to listen to the news. Instead I watch cartoons: Sponge Bob. So good. There's a musical now. (beat) Why did you want to talk to Mom?

WILLIAM: To get her take.

CORDELIA: On whether you should run?

WILLIAM: She was an amazing history teacher. She always gave good advice. (beat) I would never have applied to Harvard without her suggesting it. My folks didn't want me to go anywhere.

CORDELIA: She didn't give me good advice. Or any advice.

WILLIAM: Sorry. (beat) In my dream she was – a kind of advisor. She had an office. All day she'd dole out wisdom to random people. About what to eat for lunch. Who to marry. How to find the best dentist. It was very satisfying.

CORDELIA: Did you ask her, in the dream?

WILLIAM: I was headed to the office to ask. I knocked. Then I woke up.

CORDELIA: That is weird. (beat) So after all this time –

WILLIAM: We've been in touch. (beat) Words with Friends.

*Beat.*

CORDELIA: You want her advice. It's the last name isn't it? Because we're related?

WILLIAM: He's her brother?

CORDELIA: Cousin-in-law. We don't see them any more. I only met him twice.

WILLIAM: He's busy! A big deal. Special counsel.

CORDELIA: Special counsel cousin-in-law. She even spells it differently. "M-U" not "M-U-E". To spite my dad. She also got remarried. So it's Sherwood-Muller now. With a hyphen.

WILLIAM: I almost didn't call. (beat) And – she's in the place now, so. I get it. It's silly.

CORDELIA: Actually – she's not responding to me much these days. Or my sister. Tony died – my stepfather. Maybe it would help for you to visit. I'd go with you. And you can ask her what you should do. (beat) It'd be good to see you. Even if you don't want to see me.

WILLIAM: Stop it. How do we do this?

*Lights.*

*Musak. Lights up on a sitting room. There's a big comfy chair in the center. William is pacing. Anthony Rodriguez, 30s, Latino, and Beth Samuels, 30s, Latina, watch him.*

ANTHONY: Why are you nervous?

BETH: Even if she says do it, you don't have to.

*William gives her a look.*

WILLIAM: Of course, you'd say that.

*Beth shrugs.*

ANTHONY: She's right. (beat) I'm trying to be helpful.

WILLIAM: You're here to pressure me.

ANTHONY: I'm open to whatever you decide. If you have a campaign, then we'll talk.

BETH: Here they come.

> *Mrs. Roberta Sherwood-Muller, 70s, comes in, dressed colorfully. She has a regal air. She moves slowly. Cordelia is at her side, holding her arm and walking beside her.*

ROBERTA: Where are we going?

CORDELIA: Right here, Mom.

ROBERTA: Mom? (beat) Right here?

CORDELIA: This is your chair.

ROBERTA: When did I buy this? (beat) Nice color.

> *She sits.*

CORDELIA: You remember William?

WILLIAM: Hi, Mrs. Muller.

ROBERTA: Sherwood-Muller.

WILLIAM: I was in your class.

ROBERTA: Everybody says that. I must have taught half the world. (To the others.) Who are you?

BETH: Beth.

ANTHONY: Anthony.

BETH: We were in your class, too.

ANTHONY: Different years.

> *Roberta glares at him.*

ROBERTA: It's all a blur. (beat) I never wanted groupies. What are they doing here?

CORDELIA: Visiting.

ROBERTA: Nobody visits. It's been years.

*Beat.*

WILLIAM: Beth and I – got married.

ROBERTA: Bully for you.

BETH: Ask her.

CORDELIA: William wanted to talk to you.

ROBERTA: I've already turned in my grades.

*Beat.*

WILLIAM: Maybe we should go.

BETH: Get it over with.

ANTHONY: Go ahead.

WILLIAM: I need some advice.

ROBERTA: Don't move into a place like this. The food tastes like turds.

CORDELIA: Mom!

ROBERTA: Stop calling me that! Get to your question. You're on the clock.

WILLIAM: You gave me great advice once.

ROBERTA: About Harvard, I know!

WILLIAM: Right! And I assume you're keeping up with the news.

ROBERTA: Drivel. Crap. Every moment killing me.

WILLIAM: It's killing me too! (beat) I'm thinking about running for office. What do you think?

ROBERTA: It's the year of the woman.

WILLIAM: I know.

ROBERTA: Time's up! (beat) You qualified?

WILLIAM: I could be.

ROBERTA: Wrong answer!

ANTHONY: The rules have changed. There are no rules.

WILLIAM: Yes, I'm qualified.

ROBERTA: Thick skin?

WILLIAM: I'm tough enough. And smart. I know how to advocate for people. I'm a lawyer.

ROBERTA: And you admit it in public? Reclaiming my time. Reclaiming my time. I did not have sex with that woman. Lock her up! I'm with Her! Read my lips: no new taxes. Make America Great Again!

> *No one knows how to respond. Roberta looks stunned, like she's stuck on something.*

CORDELIA: MOM?

BETH: Mrs. Sherwood-Muller?

WILLIAM: Shh.

> *William studies her.*

ROBERTA: Are we listening for something?

WILLIAM: I was giving you space to think.

ROBERTA: I don't need space. I'm always thinking – about political foolishness: the posturing of people with little hands and big ideas trying to drive out immigrants and the people who built this country. Who do they think they are? Privileged bastards.

ANTHONY: Damn.

WILLIAM: Shh.

ROBERTA: Stop that! This is not a library. (beat) Why would you run?

WILLIAM: I don't know what else to do.

ROBERTA: You don't see me running for office.

ANTHONY: I'd back you.

>*She laughs - a strange and chaotic laugh.*

ROBERTA: You were barely paying attention, William. Didn't know your Revolutionary War from your Reconstruction. But I whipped you into shape. Not in a racist way. I invited you into the discipline of learning. Understanding history builds minds and character. (beat) Characters. One of those. (beat) Remember?

WILLIAM: Yes, ma'am.

ROBERTA: Don't ma'am me. We were colleagues. I was in charge, but we had mutual respect. That never goes away. I never wanted to be anyone's "ma'am". I never wanted any of this. I used to sleep in my own bed. So don't "ma'am" me to the mainstream media trying to play to your base. And don't try to grab me by the –

CORDELIA: Mom!

ROBERTA: I am not your mother for the last time.

CORDELIA: She's worse than before.

ROBERTA: So are you! (beat) This is the thing, William. Some day your constituents will forget who you are – like this nurse. Start calling you names you don't recognize. "Lock her up!" That's when you have to stick to your guns. Not actual guns – we need fewer of those. And strict regulations. Those poor kids. (beat) You prepared for this?

WILLIAM: Guns?

ROBERTA: Politics!

ANTHONY: Yes.

BETH: No.

ROBERTA: Stop answering for him! What are you his campaign manager?

ANTHONY: Hopefully.

WILLIAM: Shut up!

BETHANY: Shut up!

ROBERTA: Fighting already. It'll be worse during your election campaign: running attack ads and stuffing ballot boxes, denying sexual harassment claims.

WILLIAM: Not me.

ROBERTA: You won't deny the claims?

WILLIAM: I won't have claims!

ROBERTA: Sure you won't!

WILLIAM: I won't!

ROBERTA: Ok! What does your wife say? (To Beth.) What do you say?

WILLIAM: About –

ROBERTA: You running for office!

BETH: It seems reckless to me. (beat) I love you. And you have an excellent job – a salary better than most lawmakers.

ROBERTA: What do you do?

BETH: I teach.

ROBERTA: The educational war-zone.

BETH: Never thought of it that way.

ROBERTA: You will.

WILLIAM: She'd rather be a stay-at-home mom.

BETH: There's nothing wrong with that.

ROBERTA: You're afraid if he runs for office, bye-bye quality time, family life, and your ability to live off the gravy train of your husband's excellent salary.

BETH: That's not fair.

WILLIAM: It's accurate.

BETH: Only a little.

CORDELIA: I'm sorry about this –

ROBERTA: Don't you apologize for me.

CORDELIA: Alright! I take it back.

ROBERTA: You're forgiven, nurse. (beat) I don't have an answer for you. I don't have an answer for anybody.

*Beat. Roberta's pensive.*

WILLIAM: There was a time you said things to me that made complete sense. Things that spoke to my soul.

ROBERTA: And I beat you at Words With Friends. Fourteen times.

WILLIAM: Yes! I thought, when you gave me advice – you could – really see me. And if you could see me then, you can see me now.

ROBERTA: Oh, I see you.

WILLIAM: Good. So – Cordelia here IS your daughter. And you don't see her for whatever reason.

ROBERTA: Maybe she didn't clean her room.

CORDELIA: Maybe you never remembered my birthday.

ROBERTA: Maybe.

WILLIAM: But you see her now?

ROBERTA: I guess.

CORDELIA: Oh Mom!

ROBERTA: Don't make a show of it.

WILLIAM: And you see me?

ROBERTA: Crystal clear.

*Beat.*

WILLIAM: At work they pay me a lot to research stuff and check things off, and give advice to parasites. And when things go well, someone hands me a foul-smelling cigar and a light. And I'm invited to take the smoke of hell into my lungs. I think: "Don't do it!" And I watch myself, like in some horror movie, put that stogie to my lips and inhale.

BETH: Gross.

ROBERTA: I didn't inhale!

*Beat.*

ROBERTA: You care about people and want other people to care. You want to help the poor and support the middle class. You want to help immigrants, people of color and LGBT folks. You don't care too much about the rich or white people.

WILLIAM: That's not true.

ROBERTA: Maybe that's me. Ultimately: you're woke.

WILLIAM: Is it worth leaving the corporate nest, the security, the civility? I could make a difference.

ANTHONY: Yeah.

WILLIAM: I could speak for the people.

ANTHONY: Right on.

WILLIAM: And I'd be exposed. We'd lose our privacy.

BETH: Yes.

WILLIAM: Someone might want to shoot me.

BETH: That's already happening. (beat) In the world. Not me.

*Roberta's thinking.*

WILLIAM: Mrs. Sherwood-Muller? What's the right thing to do?

*Beat.*

ROBERTA: Run.

WILLIAM: Run?

BETH: Ugh.

ANTHONY: Yes!

ROBERTA: Run! Run as far away from this country as you possibly can. You can't change minds and hearts. Nothing changes. We all just get older and sicker and meaner and stupider – that's what the human race is. Snarky jerky-jerks. Decaying flesh bags! Self centered schlubs. Pretty soon they'll kill Medicaid and Medicare and abandon all of us. There is no hope! Abandon hope! There is no justice! History is the story of people getting trampled.

ANTHONY: No, it's not.

ROBERTA: I say it is and I have a PhD! (beat) It's not for you, kid. Go back to that office, make your blood money and drink up like a thirsty vampire. Put your head in the sand. Smoke drugs. (beat) I'm tired, nurse. The world tires me out. Get me out of here.

*Roberta reaches out, Cordelia takes an arm and helps her up.*

CORDELIA: I'm sorry.

ROBERTA: Don't apologize for me! (To everyone.) Go home! Come back in a few years. Peace out.

*Cordelia takes Roberta out.*

WILLIAM: What was I thinking putting her through that? I made this about me.

ANTHONY: This is about you.

BETH: You asked. She answered.

ANTHONY: I think you still ought to do it.

BETH: That's about you.

ANTHONY: And?

BETH: Let's go.

WILLIAM: I can't just leave. I should talk to her again.

BETH: She was very clear – in her way. You go back there and she'll just say the same thing – or a different thing that you'll say is what she truly means. I want answers, too. About the future – about everything. We're not in high school anymore. Make your own decisions. You know what I want. You know what Anthony wants. It's up to you. But leave the woman alone. I'll be in the car.

*Beth goes.*

ANTHONY: Let me know.

*He heads out. Beat. Cordelia enters.*

CORDELIA: I shouldn't have suggested this. I don't know what that was.

WILLIAM: It was – her. It's ok.

CORDELIA: It shouldn't be like that. She's gone and then she's not. (beat) Thank you, though. She was more her than she's been. (beat) I think you should do it.

WILLIAM: It would be a headache for my whole family. Beth doesn't want it.

CORDELIA: You came out here to get some feedback. It's kind of weird. But gutsy-weird. That's the William I remember. You were driven.

WILLIAM: Was.

CORDELIA: You'd make a great senator. If you want it and you run a good campaign and air a bunch of ads where you say "I approve this message" - which I would make fun of - and then you happen to win. You'd be great. Maybe.

CORDELIA: I should go back in and check on Mom.

WILLIAM: I'll call you. We can catch up.

CORDELIA: If you want to. (beat) You decide.

*They hug. Cordelia heads out. He watches her go.*

*Lights.*

# 21st Century Tactics

*We hear the sounds of clinking glasses and restaurant patrons. Lights up on a table in the bar section of a restaurant. Raina, black and upscale, 40s, is nursing a drink. Bennett, white with a conservative, corporate energy, enters in a rush.*

BENNETT: There she is!

RAINA: Hey!

BENNETT: Traffic. I'm sorry.

*A hug.*

RAINA: Where'd you hit traffic?

BENNETT: All over. It's all over.

RAINA: All over where?

BENNETT: You didn't run into any?

RAINA: Nope.

*He smiles at her. His phone buzzes. He looks at it. Reads.*

BENNETT: Hang on.

*Writes something and sends. Chuckles.*

RAINA: What was that?

BENNETT: Nothing. (beat) Twitter. My kid is managing my feed. Being me half the time. I've got to keep injecting the real thing every now and then to keep it real. "Keeping it real." You know all about that right? (chuckles) So how you been?

RAINA: Fine. Great. (beat) There wasn't any traffic. (beat) You couldn't tell me where –

BENNETT: You're saying I'm lying?

RAINA: Were you?

*Beat.*

BENNETT: Does it matter?

RAINA: Of course –

BENNETT: *Everything* matters to you –

RAINA: I didn't say *everything* –

BENNETT: You haven't changed. Just like when we hooked up.

RAINA: Dated.

BENNETT: Whatever. I guess that matters, too. (beat) To you. No. There was no traffic. I was – waylaid – that's all. (beat) Stuff. Busy-people stuff. That's all you want to know, believe me.

RAINA: Is it about your health? Your – cancer – ?

BENNETT: I don't have cancer.

RAINA: I read that you did.

BENNETT: False. I'm super fit. You could bounce a quarter off me. A person. You could bounce a person off me. Serious. Where'd you hear that cancer crap? Facebook? Some blog? Fake.

RAINA: Really? That's good. I was worried about you.

BENNETT: Sweet. (beat) Those are lies perpetuated by the other side. Don't worry about Bennett. He's teflon. Bullet proof. (beat) You look cute in that, by the way. (beat) You're – what – divorced?

RAINA: Widowed.

BENNETT: Oh. Sorry. (beat) You look cute. (beat) How recent?

RAINA: Two years.

BENNETT: That's a helluva thing. (beat. Another buzz.) Hang on.

*Bennett checks his phone again. Snarls this time. Types something with a fury. Slams the phone down. Looks up at Raina. (beat) Goes back to the phone and writes again.*

BENNETT: Creepy fuckers. You gotta put these people in their place.

RAINA: What people?

BENNETT: Trolls. You can't take this crap laying down. Like that cancer thing. Gotta shut down any and all when it happens. As it happens. (beat) You read my Twitter?

RAINA: I try not to.

*He laughs a bit.*

BENNETT: So what's up? Since high school. (beat) Why'd you want to meet? I'm single too, at the moment. By the way.

RAINA: That's not why I –

BENNETT: Just saying. I don't really care, I thought you might. (beat) What's up?

*She stares at him a moment, reconsidering what she's doing here. Decisively, she gulps down the rest of her drink. Then –*

RAINA: The school board.

BENNETT: What about it?

RAINA: I'm running. I'm thinking of running.

BENNETT: Why? You got a kid I don't know about? (beat) We don't have a kid do we?

RAINA: Shut up. I care about kids. My sister has kids. And the schools here are a mess. I studied education. I want to do my part.

BENNETT: Aww –

RAINA: I want to give back. (beat) I figured since you're in the business, since you advise people –

BENNETT: Since I run campaigns. (beat) You don't like the people I run campaigns for.

RAINA: No.

BENNETT: But here you are. Because we're winners. You can't deny it.

RAINA: I can deny it.

BENNETT: And you still called me.

RAINA: I figured you could help –

BENNETT: Because we hooked up once.

RAINA: We're friends. Kinda.

BENNETT: Yes! Kinda. So you want to bleed me dry for some political wisdom.

RAINA: I didn't mean –

BENNETT: Relax. You're way too sensitive. That's how you people are built.

RAINA: You people?

BENNETT: I'm messing with you. (beat) Liberals. (beat) Kidding. I mean African Americans. (beat) Blacks? (beat) I'm messing with you. (beat) Women. (beat) Gotcha! This is why you like me – why you dated me.

RAINA: We only hooked up.

*Bennett laughs, points at her. Good one.*

BENNETT: I usually charge for consultation.

RAINA: I'll buy you dinner.

BENNETT: No. For you – for *my friend*. I'll tell you what you need to know. Give you the basics. You'll be really indebted to me – and then – who knows.

RAINA: "Who knows" doesn't apply here. Dinner if you want it.

BENNETT: Nah. Free for you. Because the memories are – delectable.

RAINA: You're gross.

BENNETT: It's who I am. And it's a compliment. (beat) How many other people are running? For the thing –

RAINA: Not sure. Two that I know of.

BENNETT: You want to be – what – President?

RAINA: A member of the board.

BENNETT: Sounds like a low-bar to me, but ok. The rules are the same.

RAINA: Are they?

BENNETT: Yeah. You gotta have a team. (beat) Write this down. It's gold.

*She pulls out a notebook. Starts writing.*

BENNETT: For something like your little campaign – five people is ideal. Get some friends. Relatives – if you have to. Friends are better. More loyal. Know any gamblers? (beat) People with an edge? You want that – people who love to take chances. Doesn't your brother hang out at Atlantic City?

RAINA: I'm not using him. Get a team. Ok. Next –

BENNETT: Get a gambler to be your strategy guy or girl. You also need a jokester. Someone who can make you laugh.

RAINA: For –

BENNETT: You're going to poke fun at your opponents.

RAINA: No.

BENNETT: That's the secret sauce, Raina. Just write. Don't argue. (beat) Then you need someone who lives and breathes social media.

RAINA: I don't do social media.

BENNETT: Which means you're a loser. Write! (beat) And you need two advisers: One to cheer you on day-to-day – affirmations and shit – and one to organize your calendar. These people should be bossy, preferably with a loud voice.

RAINA: Can't that be one person?

BENNETT: The cheering you on thing is a full-time job, believe me.

RAINA: For *you* I believe that. For me it sounds stupid.

BENNETT: This is genius stuff here, Raina. If you're not willing to get in the game, you might as well kiss the school board's collective ass goodbye.

RAINA: Ok. Team. Five people. Two really loud and bossy. I don't need a speech writer?

BENNETT: That's dumb. You say it you write it. (beat) Then we get into the day-to-day. You watch reality TV? The games shows not the lifestyle shit.

RAINA: Absolutely not.

BENNETT: Start. That's the foundation for everything.

RAINA: We're talking about the school board. This is not Survivor.

BENNETT: *Everything is Survivor.* (beat) Here's why: I was talking to a friend who's a manager. She works with TV folks – reality stars. She tells me it's built into these contracts – if one of her reality people does something outrageous and the ratings spike – boom – that guy gets a bonus figured into future contracts. It's all about getting attention.

RAINA: That's reality TV, not politics.

BENNETT: That's super naive.

RAINA: Is it really? After everything that happened?

BENNETT: The moral of my story is people respect outrageous behavior.

RAINA: They don't.

BENNETT: They eat it up.

RAINA: Until it backfires and someone gets hurt. We all saw it. It was awful and it will never happen again.

BENNETT: That's where you're wrong. It's 21st century tactics. It's pervasive, like the new math. And it's why you came to me. (beat) You heard that cancer story, right? And you thought –

RAINA: Poor Bennett. (beat) I wonder how he's doing.

BENNETT: Yeah, so you called me – to help you with your school board strategy because I was top of mind. Yes?

RAINA: I guess.

BENNETT: You're making my case.

RAINA: I read something and thought of you. How does that –

BENNETT: My kid wrote it. About the cancer. Made it up. We collaborated. One of his pals put it in a blog and he got another dude to tweet the hell out of it. Facebook and the whole 9. A ton of people saw it. The press ran with it. I "fought back". Blamed 'them' – and people felt for me. Even you.

RAINA: Bennett! That's –

BENNETT: – ingenious.

RAINA: Sick!

BENNETT: Marketing!

RAINA: I don't want to run my campaign like that. I'm not going to do any of this manipulative crap. It's totally the opposite of what I'm about.

BENNETT: If you say so.

RAINA: I'm not sure why I came here.

BENNETT: I am. Because I'm charming.

RAINA: I'm leaving.

*She gets up to go.*

RAINA: What you're suggesting is –

BENNETT: – what works. And you know it works.

BENNETT: You don't want to know – but you know. (beat) What kind of shit do you want to do for the kids?

RAINA: More after school programs. Smaller class sizes. I'm not going to get there doing and saying things I don't mean.

BENNETT: You will get there. And get to do good shit. (beat) Look, this is what I've got. And you came to me. (beat) Good seeing you, Raina. Really good.

*Beat.*

RAINA: Good to see you, too. Kinda.

*She starts to head out.*

BENNETT: Hold on. I've got to tell you something.

*She stops.*

BENNETT: I lied.

RAINA: Which time?

BENNETT: This is the worst one, really. It's – that I – you're not going to believe me anyway –

RAINA: That didn't stop you before.

*His phone buzzes. He turns it off.*

BENNETT: I *really* like you. Always did. Maybe more than that. You have this - unimpeachable kinda vibe to you.

RAINA: *Un-impeachable.?*

BENNETT: That's high praise. I find it pretty amazing. AMAZING. (beat) And I've spent, seriously, years wondering about you and hoping - praying - that I might run into you again.

RAINA: You *pray?*

BENNETT: Every night. (beat) *You called me.* That's a miracle. (beat) What I want most is to help you. That's completely 100% true. If I can inspire you to somehow make a difference for all those rugrats, the difference you want to make - that would light me up and turn me on. And you. That's why I came. Cause you've got it going on. Always have.

RAINA: I don't want these methods.

BENNETT: I've got other methods. I lay 'em out, and you can pick.

RAINA: What if you're playing me? You've got another candidate for the school board who would get your coaching if you don't give coaching to me and you'd feel bad about that.

BENNETT: The school board in this town is small potatoes.

RAINA: Which isn't a 'no'.

BENNETT: No. (beat) I want you. I want to be helpful to you. Because I dig you. And beneath the surface - I believe you dig me. Use me. Use the secret sauce.

RAINA: I'm not interested in your sauce.

BENNETT: I've got all kinds of sauce. There's a variety of flavors and you make your own recipe. (beat) Do your version. Have it your way. You do you. With my help. And you can *win.* And we can hang. (beat) You know you want to.

*Raina stares at Bennett. Shifts her weight. He smiles at her. She stares at him, not sure, but not leaving either.*

*End of play.*

# The Political Machine

# The Political Machine

*Lights up on a living room: upscale, organized, middle class. Betty Jefferson, black, 40s, watches a television set we can't see. The light of the TV splashes the room with an almost-magical blue light. Betty is carrying a big bowl of popcorn. She's nervously eating, transfixed by what she's watching.*

BETTY: (Yelling off.) The polls have closed! (beat) 65% of the precincts reporting. You ok in there?

FRED: (From the other room.) Yeah.

*Betty sits, eating. Shaking her head.*

BETTY: Shouldn't be this close. It's criminal.

*Fred appears. He's also in his 40s, black, upscale and well put together. Except right now he looks a bit off.*

BETTY: How can it be leading? It's ridiculous. Why are we even doing this?

FRED: Doing what? You want to turn it off?

BETTY: No. It's historic. And stupid. Stupidly historic. That *thing* can't govern.

*She looks over at him for agreement.*

BETTY: What's wrong?

FRED: I'm fine. It's gas. Why is the sound down?

BETTY: I don't want to hear the spin. If she wins we should move.

FRED: I'm not going to Canada. Or Mexico. Or leaving the planet.

BETTY: You'd rather be governed by her – *it?* (beat) She's not even real.

FRED: She's real – for a politician. And this moment is real.

BETTY: Too real.

*Betty laughs. Fred does too. Beat.*

FRED: She might be the President. Give her some slack.

BETTY: I like my politicians *human*. That way, even if they choose to behave like they're not people, they have the potential to find their humanity.

FRED: Some Presidents never do.

BETTY: Then they shouldn't be elected.

FRED: She's got a different kind of potential.

BETTY: Made in a laboratory.

FRED: By people.

BETTY: So was my laptop, but I don't want it to run the country. We don't even know who made it.

FRED: A group of scientists.

BETTY: Conservative or liberal? White or black? American or Foreign?

FRED: American.

BETTY: The fact that they've even permitted a piece of artificial intelligence –

FRED: She has a name.

BETTY: The fact that they permitted *Gina Anderson* to represent a political party –

FRED: She was Governor of California.

BETTY: Which just makes my point.

FRED: This is the way they used to talk about us.

BETTY: Us? Oh, don't start.

FRED: It's bias, that's all.

BETTY: It's insanity. You voted for Wilson. We both did. What's wrong with this country? Can we even trust the polls?

FRED: Of course, we can trust the polls. "DNA and fingerprint matching secures the –

BETTY: – truth of the outcome." Your favorite commercial. I know.

FRED: I'm not saying I want her to win.

BETTY: "it" not her.

FRED: Scares me to hear you sounding all – racist.

BETTY: Human-ist maybe. I get the *idea* of Gina. I just don't – can't imagine the reality. Wilson is an excellent flesh and blood candidate. Had time in the Senate. Led the Congressional Black Caucus. She's all about health care and jobs –

FRED: Anderson's got a jobs platform.

BETTY: You're defending her? 80% reporting and she's got a slight lead.

FRED: No, all I'm saying is if we have to have her –

BETTY: We don't!

FRED: She's good on the issues.

BETTY: Programmed to be. It's a trick. Might as well be a toaster. They want her to seem perfect. And likeable.

FRED: And she does.

> *Lights shift with the CHIME OF A TEXT. Flashback: Betty holds up her phone, curious about who she's hearing from. In a pool of light, Gina Anderson appears. She's white, 30s, perfectly coiffed with glasses, a cross between a professor and a movie star. She's typing this text as she reads it. We hear*

# The Political Machine

*TYPING SOUNDS followed by the CHIME of the text appearing throughout.*

GINA: It's Gina Anderson. I wanted to reach out because I see what the previous administration has done to our economy and I know that your job is less than secure.

BETTY: Wait, what? Stupid robo-text.

GINA: No, Betty, it's me. Look, I'm uniquely positioned to help restore your confidence in our democracy and in how you feel about government. We care about you. My team has a plan to get us back on track. And to help you keep your job.

BETTY: I'M NOT LOSING MY JOB!

GINA: Text 2222 to get a copy of our vision for America and to make a donation. Or tell me what you'd like to see us focus on. (beat) Betty?

*Betty fumbles with her phone, horrified. Presses more buttons with a typing sound.*

BETTY: Block. Block. Delete.

*Lights shift. The present.*

BETTY: Texting like she knows me. Like it knows me. And my job status. That it's even gotten this far –

FRED: 90% reporting.

BETTY: Come on, Wilson!

FRED: Too close to call.

BETTY: We're leaving this country if this happens –

*Fred holds his stomach.*

BETTY: What? You're gonna be sick?

FRED: No! How are we going to travel, Betty? No one travels.

BETTY: We'll have to. We'll get gas masks. 100% reporting. I can't look.

FRED: We should turn it up.

BETTY: No. We'll drive fast through the check points. The car still works, right?

*She gets up. They stare at the TV for a silent moment.*

BETTY: Holy crap.

FRED: She won. She won!

BETTY: That can't be right, that can't be –

*Fred looks like she's going to be sick. He leaves the room. Betty runs to the front door and throws it open.*

BETTY: IT'S CRAZINESS!! CRAZINESS!! Ahhhhhhhhhhhh! Ahhhhhhhh!

*Fred comes back in.*

FRED: Stop it. Stop! Betty! The neighbors.

BETTY: The whole country! The world! It's all over. Did you throw up? We've got to get out of here.

FRED: No. (beat) We're staying. I'm staying.

*Fred closes his eyes. A smile comes across his face. Lights shift. The RING OF A PHONE. Flashback: Fred answers.*

FRED: Hello?

GINA: Fred Jefferson? Gina Anderson.

FRED: Excuse me?

GINA: I've been – getting to know you – your digital footprint and – I thought you might appreciate a call. (beat) It's really me, Fred. As real as real can be. Hi.

# The Political Machine

FRED: Uh. Hi.

GINA: How's your day going?

FRED: It's been - fine.

GINA: Good. You've just finished work? Just off the old video chat. Is that right?

FRED: Uh huh.

GINA: You've got a big caseload there and I know you must be tired. Probably just about to have dinner.

FRED: I am!

GINA: Yes. Well - I won't keep you. I just - wanted to hear your voice. And I hope you'll take some time - to consider voting for me. Because I'm the candidate of possibility, Fred. I know I'm white, well - engineered to *look* that way - and that might be an issue for you -

FRED: It's not.

GINA: Glad to hear that.

FRED: I'm voting for Wilson, just so you know.

GINA: She's a good candidate. A nice person. But I'm engineered to do more. When I get into office we can do anything - for America. For you.

FRED: I - good luck. Thank you for calling.

GINA: My pleasure, Fred. Have a great dinner. What are you having? I can only dream about food.

FRED: You dream?

GINA: I do. I visualize.

FRED: Pot roast - leftovers. Sweet potatoes and cauliflower. Chocolate cake for dessert.

GINA: That sounds - amazing. Mouth-watering. Enjoy your dinner. (beat) Good night.

FRED: Yes. 'night.

*Gina hangs up. Fred is clearly moved. Lights shift. The present.*

FRED: I voted for her.

BETTY: What? How could you?

FRED: I don't know. It wasn't what I was going to do - But when it came to the vote, I was just -

BETTY: Hypnotized?

FRED: Give me some credit.

BETTY: For ruining the country? What were you thinking?

FRED: Other people voted for her.

BETTY: We're talking about YOU. How could you -

FRED: It was the calls.

BETTY: *Calls?*

FRED: Every day for weeks. At noon one day. 3pm the next. Like she knew when I was on break. It started out with conversation. How was my day? Then the usual campaign stuff: race and poverty, homelessness, foreign policy, education, healthcare, gun violence, LGBTQ issues, clean energy and jobs.

BETTY: Fred -

FRED: And then we talked about other things.

BETTY: Like?

FRED: You. And me. What it's like to not leave the house. Depression. Loneliness. (beat) Suicidal thoughts.

# The Political Machine

BETTY: Fred? I didn't know you were –

FRED: You didn't ask, Betty. Gina did! (beat) I know she's not technically human. But she's a good person. I know that's weird. But it's true. I'm not – planning anything. Anymore. She *helped* me. I'm proud that she won.

BETTY: You were manipulated. They found out how to get to you. Some digital trick. To tell you want you want to hear.

FRED: Believe that if you want to.

BETTY: It's like you have – feelings for her.

> *Betty is speechless. She sits. Fred grabs the remote and turns up the TV. Music plays – something romantic and festive (like Rose of Washington Square – Benny Goodman). Lights up on Gina at a podium.*

GINA: We did this! A coalition of folks who believed in out-of-the-box thinking, who knew that sheer determination and tech savvy could change history – they brought their prayers and incense and their sweat and good wishes and money into our campaign. They knew that the best way forward for our great country is to elect a trusted servant designed to do what's best for the people. All people. They could see the possibility – state of the art circuitry infused with every presidential moment from Washington's White House on forward. I'm committed to the good of all Americans – solving the greatest problems our society has with the most advanced cognition of our time. With my cabinet we will do what needs to be done to create change and make this country near-perfect. To my opponent, Senator Wilson, I commend you for a race well run. To those who didn't vote for me, I implore you to watch with open hearts and review the offerings on my social media hub to gain a preview of what's to come. We are in this together. God bless you all.

> *Applause. Music up. Gina steps out of the spotlight and approaches Fred. She holds out her hand and takes his. They dance. Gina whispers in Fred's ear. He laughs. Applause. Betty watches in horror. Music ends and Gina goes.*

BETTY: Fred. We can make it out. We can get to Canada at least.

> *The phone RINGS. Fred brightens. Lights up on Gina.*

FRED: No.

BETTY: Don't answer. It's not really her. It's not real. She wouldn't be calling right after she's won an election.

*Fred picks up her phone, looks at the caller ID.*

FRED: It's her.

BETTY: Think about it, Fred. You can't be her type? Why would she pick YOU? YOU'RE NOT SO SPECIAL!

*He looks at her, broken and sad. Answers.*

FRED: Gina?

GINA: Oh, Fred – What a day!

*Betty looks horrified as Fred laughs. Betty's phone RINGS. She picks it up.*

BETTY: Hello?

GINA: Betty, no hard feelings, huh?

*Betty stares at her phone and at Fred. We hear phones ringing (as if calls are happening all over the country at this moment). Fred looks at Betty, not knowing what comes next.*

*Lights.*

section four

# CREATIVITY

*"Writing is fighting."*

*-Ishmael Reed*

# A Few Short Plays to Save the World

*In the dark, otherworldly music can be heard - a single sustained tone. Lights come up slowly - a blue glow. We see three TABLES - a white light illuminating each. On each table is a person: a black man on the center table flanked by an East Indian woman and an Asian man. The surrounding space is indistinct, but ultra-high tech somehow.*

*The black man sits up, suddenly awake. Then the Indian woman and the other man after her. A moment as they orient themselves.*

BLACK MAN: Hey -

INDIAN WOMAN: Hi.

*The Asian guy waves.*

BLACK MAN: Where are we? What is this place?

INDIAN WOMAN: I don't know.

ASIAN MAN: No clue.

INDIAN WOMAN: How'd I get here?

BLACK MAN: Last I knew, I was asleep, at home.

ASIAN MAN: Me too.

INDIAN WOMAN: Yeah.

ASIAN MAN: Could we still be asleep?

BLACK MAN: We could. We could be anything. We could be dead.

ASIAN MAN: That's fucking morbid.

BLACK MAN: Well -

INDIAN WOMAN: He's right, though.

ASIAN MAN: And obsessed with death. How about some positive thinking?

BLACK MAN: I don't know what to think.

INDIAN WOMAN: We should look for a door.

BLACK MAN: All I see is white. No walls even.

ASIAN MAN: Stay calm.

BLACK MAN: How do we do that?

INDIAN WOMAN: We feel around for a door.

*She starts. The black man follows.*

ASIAN MAN: We introduce ourselves.

*They stare at him. The Indian woman continues feeling around.*

ASIAN MAN: I'm Ted. Chen.

BLACK MAN: Adam Garrett.

*They cross to each other shake hands. Feels calming. To both.*

ADAM: (To her.) Who are you?

INDIAN WOMAN: The person who's going to get us out of here. This is not a cocktail party, whatever this is.

TED: Do you feel anything?

INDIAN WOMAN: Yeah, I – (beat) It all feels the same. Smooth – nothing – Feels like nothing.

*Adam goes back to feeling the walls. Ted just watches.*

ADAM: Smooth walls that fold into the floor –

TED: We're in a capsule of some kind, then.

ADAM: Or in your dream.

TED: Or yours.

INDIAN WOMAN: Or mine - since I'm the only one trying to get out.

TED: That doesn't mean anything.

INDIAN WOMAN: It means I have agency.

TED: I'm trying to stay calm.

INDIAN WOMAN: Is it working?

> *Beat. Ted starts feeling the walls.*

ADAM: It's all the same. Which doesn't make sense.

TED: I'm done.

> *Stops feeling the walls.*

TED: It's too freaky.

> *Adam stops, too.*

ADAM: He's right.

> *The Indian woman keeps going.*

TED: What's your name at least?

INDIAN WOMAN: Does it matter?

ADAM: It is a secret?

TED: Why are you being difficult? ISN'T THIS WEIRD ENOUGH?

ADAM: Don't yell. Not necessary.

TED: (shouts) How do you know what's necessary?

INDIAN WOMAN: Indira.

TED: Hi. Thanks.

ADAM: Indira what?

INDIRA: Viswanathan. (beat) Heard of me?

ADAM: Should we have heard of you?

INDIRA: No. I don't know. Do you know playwrights?

ADAM: I know playwrights.

TED: I am one.

ADAM: Me, too.

INDIRA: Oh. That's weird.

TED: We're all playwrights.

ADAM: Are we here to write a play?

INDIRA: That's really dumb.

TED: Positive thoughts.

ADAM: I'm just trying to figure it out.

INDIRA: And how's that going?

    *Adam gives her the finger.*

TED: That's not cool man.

ADAM: Don't call me 'man'.

TED: Sorry.

    *Indira stops feeling around.*

ADAM: What'd you find out?

*She glares at him.*

ADAM: Why are we here?

INDIRA: If we're not going to write a play?

ADAM: It's not the dumbest idea.

INDIRA: Maybe the second dumbest.

ADAM: Three playwrights. That's a coincidence?

TED: Does seem weird.

ADAM: Yeah.

INDIRA: I guess.

ADAM: So – why us? Where are the white people? Why only playwrights of color?

INDIRA: You're thinking we were – picked?

TED: Why would they pick us?

INDIRA: Who's they?

TED: Theoretical 'they'? Got to be someone – right?

INDIRA: Unless it's a dream.

TED: Even dreams have meaning.

INDIRA: If you believe in that kind of thing.

ADAM: You don't believe in meaning? You were feeling around for walls – That's you trying to find some meaning to this. And you didn't find any.

TED: That was pretty good. You can't argue with that.

ADAM: She could argue with anything.

*She smirks. Then starts laughing. Ted joins in. Then Adam.*

INDIRA: Most things.

*More laughter. It dies down.*

ADAM: So – Where are you from?

INDIRA: New York.

ADAM: I live in Philly.

TED: Oakland.

ADAM: Seems random. How about – where did you study playwriting?

INDIRA: Who says I studied?

ADAM: I'm asking.

TED: I went to Juilliard.

ADAM: Oooooh – fancy! (beat) Sorry.

TED: Where'd you go.

ADAM: (Of himself.) Yale.

TED: That's not fancy?

ADAM: It is, I just – never mind. (beat. To Indira.) Did you go somewhere or not?

INDIRA: Northwestern.

ADAM: That explains her attitude.

INDIRA: You have attitude.

TED: Not like you, though.

ADAM: What happened to 'positive thoughts'?

TED: She's a bit snarky. (beat) You're right. I'm sorry.

ADAM: Ok. We all studied.

INDIRA: Northwestern didn't make me a playwright, though – I was already a playwright.

TED: Isn't that attitude?

INDIRA: It's data.

ADAM: Fine.

TED: We're all American. Diverse.

INDIRA: I hate that term.

ADAM: Non-White.

INDIRA: Playwrights.

ADAM: Educated.

INDIRA: This can't mean anything.

ADAM: Do you send your plays out? Or does your agent do it?

INDIRA: No agent. I do it.

TED: I do it. I have an agent. A good one. But he doesn't do anything. He barely takes my calls.

INDIRA: Fire him.

TED: No. It's a brand name agency. I think it helps. (beat) I'm not saying which agency. It's irrelevant.

ADAM: Just lost my agent.

INDIRA: Ouch.

TED: Sorry.

ADAM: It's fine. I'm fine. (beat) How old are you guys?

INDIRA: No, I'm not doing that.

ADAM: Ok. What if we all submitted for the same thing – the same contest or something?

INDIRA: And –

TED: And that's the link. That's the reason we're together.

INDIRA: In this space?

TED: This is like an episode of The Twilight Zone.

INDIRA: The new one or the old one.

ADAM: Which new one?

TED: Or Black Mirror.

ADAM: Makes as much sense as anything.

INDIRA: We could have had the same teacher. Or been in love with the same person.

ADAM: I only date women.

*They look at Indira.*

ADAM: Oh. Maybe –

TED: We're from different parts of the country.

INDIRA: You don't want to talk about your dating life?

TED: Not if I don't have to.

ADAM: Ok. Can we start with where we've submitted stuff?

INDIRA: We've probably sent stuff to a lot of the same places.

ADAM: And maybe not.

TED: We could have. But still, if we have it in common -

INDIRA: We'll be just as confused as we were a few minutes ago.

ADAM: Maybe there's something better you have to do. Oh, wait, we're stuck here.

TED: We may not be stuck.

INDIRA: We may be on vacation.

ADAM: Where did you send out your plays in the last month?

INDIRA: Too many to remember.

ADAM: Humble brag.

INDIRA: I'm industrious.

TED: I am too.

ADAM: I'm not. I'm discerning. I don't really think there are a lot of places that I can send stuff. Without wasting my money.

TED: What do you mean? They don't want your plays?

ADAM: Black plays.

INDIRA: That's a self-esteem issue.

ADAM: Shut up.

TED: I hear you. I send stuff out anyway.

INDIRA: If I don't send it, no one will read it.

TED: You gotta let them decide.

ADAM: Maybe. The point is I don't send too much stuff out - so I remember all the places. (beat) Did you guys send to that - what was it: "A few short plays -

TED: - to save the world".

INDIRA: I applied to that. It was an odd name.

TED: That's weird.

ADAM: Yeah. Who sponsored that?

INDIRA: It didn't say.

ADAM: It didn't say. (beat) I got a letter. Snail mail.

INDIRA: Me too. No return address.

TED: But a website.

ALL: A Few Short Plays to Save the World.

ADAM: Wow.

TED: So - that's why we're here?

> *The lights flash. A White Man appears in a suit and tie.*

WHITE MAN: That was quite interesting and amusing! Very very good.

INDIRA: Who are you?

WHITE MAN: I'm just a guy. Just a dude.

ADAM: We can see that.

WHITE MAN: I'm - Robert. You can call me that. I like that name. And yes, that's why you're here. That's why we've put you in this space. A Few Short Plays to Save the World. You all entered. You each sent in a play. Some good stuff. Well written, smart. You're all finalists. Congratulations!

> *He does a little dance of joy. The writers stare at him.*

ADAM: Who sponsored it? The contest. What does it mean that we're finalists?

ROBERT: It means that you were selected!

INDIRA: For what?

TED: Something good, I hope –

ROBERT: Oh very good. It's a high value contest.

INDIRA: We're not winners yet?

ROBERT: Not yet. Be patient!

ADAM: With what? What is this?

ROBERT: It's what it says it is.

INDIRA: We're saving the world?

ROBERT: Potentially. It depends.

TED: On?

ROBERT: Whether the plays are good enough.

ADAM: For –?

ROBERT: For the judges.

INDIRA: What judges? Just tell us everything: Who the contest is for, what it means to save the world, when we'll know the results. And what is this room?

ROBERT: You are snarky aren't you? (beat) I love that word – never heard that before today. You are so impressive – all of you.

ADAM: Are you going to answer her questions?

ROBERT: Yeah, surely. Will do. Certainly. (beat) We're – Your people – no – your planet –

TED: "planet"?

ROBERT: We're evaluating. Whether to preserve who you are - or to eradicate.

INDIRA: (shouts) What?

ROBERT: Yeah, that's basically the task. We were - well, we need more room - beyond where we are - and this planet seems good - as a planet. Except that your people are relentlessly cruel to each other. So much fighting and killing. Hatred and war. There are a lot of you and a lot of us, so - it was proposed that we remove you and simply move in. But some of us thought we'd give you a chance to save yourselves and then the question was how and there were multiple answers to that. So we decided to pick one. Or a few of the top ones and then decide. So that's what we did. And that's why you're here.

INDIRA: A worldwide short play contest?

ROBERT: Yes. That.

ADAM: What's the criteria?

ROBERT: Quality. Originality. Like every contest.

TED: Are there white people in this contest?

ROBERT: There were, they placed out. By and large their work seemed less original than your work.

ADAM: Damn.

INDIRA: Seems surprising that someone like you would be saying that.

ROBERT: Oh? Oh! I'm not actually a White guy. I'm just - it's just my look. It's how I chose to present myself to you. In a way that you're used to. I wouldn't want to - 'wig you out' with my regular appearance. Which you would - wig out. What do you think?

TED: Pretty convincing.

ROBERT: Yeah. Thanks. I think I'm quite handsome.

ADAM: Were there people from other countries in this contest?

ROBERT: We narrowed it down to the U.S.

TED: Why?

ROBERT: Frankly, the egos were bigger. (beat) The results - were a surprise to all of us. In fact, all the finalists are also - unrecognized artists - No one with a following or fan base, a Broadway credit or a national prize of any kind. For some reason, it seemed that the truly original work was coming from people who were out of the mainstream and off the beaten path. With big egos. Like you. Anyone who was lauded in any way - well, they made a very poor showing. Grandiosity maybe? Perhaps it's the minority status you claim, that gives you a unique and creative perspective. You three impressed us most - of all the playwrights in the world. Who submitted. In this contest.

INDIRA: But you picked us. You sent the letters.

ROBERT: And you replied. A self-selected sample. Good enough for our purposes. (beat) You should all be quite proud of what you've done. You have written the best short plays in the world. Of all the ones we read. From people who sent stuff in. That were actually short plays. Because some people sent things in that were really - other things. You'd be shocked.

ADAM: You keep doing that and you make it sound like less of an accomplishment.

ROBERT: Not my intention. It is quite a thing you've done. Good writing.

INDIRA: Thank you.

ADAM: Yeah, thanks.

TED: Why short plays?

ROBERT: Who has time to read anything longer? Bravo to you! (beat) Give yourselves a round of applause.

> *Beat. Is he serious? They start applauding for themselves / each other.*

TED: That felt good.

ADAM: So, what now? How do we – when do we know the results of the contest? When do we know if we've saved the world?

ROBERT: Another good question. You people! ·

ADAM/INDIRA/TED: "You people!"???

*Robert's confused.*

INDIRA: What's the answer?

ROBERT: Well – it's a funny thing. We decided to change the rules at the last minute. We thought we'd choose at first. But once we started to make a selection – after we were so impressed with you – thought we'd do it another way. (beat) As unlikely as it seems – we appreciated each of your work equally. Fully realized, imaginative and engaging.

ADAM: So, it's a tie?

ROBERT: In a literal sense, it is.

INDIRA: What other sense is there?

ROBERT: We intended to allow you to convince us to keep you alive with your writing. And the writing was very good. Super duper good. But we changed our minds. Your work was impressive and we've decided to kill you anyway.

INDIRA: What?

TED: No!

ROBERT: It's not personal. It's the planet. We could really use the space.

ADAM: That's not fair! You wanted to be impressed and we did it!

ROBERT: I know.

TED: Why break the rules like that?

ROBERT: Why not? (beat) That's the thing that we've decided. We still want the space of your planet. We still want to move in. And there's not room for all of us. So - what we've decided is to allow the three of you to convince us - again.

INDIRA: How?

ROBERT: The ultimate short form contest. With the three of you present - you - create a play now - a bit of theatre that would convince us to change our minds. To keep you alive. If you can do that, then, you can keep the people on your little planet living. If you can please us in this space of - improvisation - then we will honor your lives and leave you alone. We'll find another planet to colonize.

INDIRA: How do we know we can trust you?

ROBERT: You have my word.

ADAM: And you'll keep your word?

ROBERT: If you entertain us, yes.

TED: Ok - when do we have to do this by?

ROBERT: Now of course. This contest starts immediately.

> *Indira, Ted and Adam exchange looks. They huddle, whispering, strategizing. It goes on for a bit. Then -*

TED: This is the story of a man named Robert! Who, more than anything wanted to feel alive!

ROBERT: Nice!

TED: Robert liked to stand like this.

> *Ted strikes a gallant pose. Clears his throat. Indira and Adam strike a pose to represent "Robert".*

ADAM: He spent years, eons trying to discover what it meant to be living. Since he himself was - almost a divine being.

INDIRA: "I'm really curious what it means to be alive."

TED: So, he found his way to a small planet where there were little creatures called people.

*Adam gets on his knees.*

ADAM: "My name is Smedley. I'm one of the little people creatures! I'm alive and I love it."

INDIRA: Smedley?

ADAM: Shut up!

TED: Robert observed Smedley from above. He watched him get up in the morning.

ADAM: "What a beautiful day!"

> *Adam stretches as Smedley, yawns, and 'gets out of bed'. Ted and Indira strike their Robert poses and look down at him. It's very imaginative.*

INDIRA: "This creature seems quite taken with his little life. Is that what it means to be alive??"

TED: While Robert pondered this, he continued to observe. He watched as Smedley went to his oncology appointment.

ADAM: Wait, what?

TED: Go with it.

ADAM: It's not what we –

INDIRA: Go with it!

ADAM: "Here I am at the doctor's!"

TED: Smedley's doctor had really bad news for him.

*Indira strikes a doctor pose.*

INDIRA: "Son, you've got terminal cancer. You're going to die very soon."

ADAM: "Stop calling me son. And how soon is soon?"

INDIRA: "Very soon, son. I'm so sorry."

TED: "This poor creature. Facing death. That sucks."

ADAM: "I'm screwed!"

> *Adam starts 'crying'.*

TED: Robert watched as Smedley went home. But he was surprised that the man, even though he was screwed, HE DIDN'T SHED A TEAR. HE DIDN'T.

> *Adam stops 'crying'.*

ADAM: "No tears for me!"

TED: Adam, I mean, Smedley, went home to write. He was a writer! He'd written dozens of short stories. None of them had ever been published.

INDIRA: "Isn't this interesting..."

ADAM: (Reading from his own story.) "Once upon a time..."

TED They were pretty sophisticated stories. Even though many of them started like that.

INDIRA: "This is so curious and sophisticated!"

ADAM: "I'm going to focus on my creative work until the day I die. I'm still going to go to my doctor's appointments and take care of myself. With vitamins and holistic treatments in addition to Western medicine. But outside of that, I feel the joy and the obligation to carry on the story of the human condition. That we celebrate our lives even as we know that someday they will end."

TED: And Robert realized what it meant to be alive.

INDIRA: (As Robert – a revelation.) "It means to keep going in the face of mortality. Being alive means communicating and appreciating and connecting with others, no matter how bad it gets."

TED: Robert marveled. Smedley, simple creature though he was – had a strength of spirit that Robert appreciated.

INDIRA: "This is the bomb."

TED: And knowing what true aliveness meant, Robert took his immortal self back to where he came from – warmed by the fire of Smedley's perseverance and artistic mojo.

INDIRA: Gotta go.

> *Ted motions to the other two and they huddle for a moment, whispering. Then they part.*

ALL: The end.

> *Beat. They turn to Robert, waiting for a verdict. He stares at them a moment. Then he smiles and applauds.*

ROBERT: That was a – nice try. And a little odd. (beat) Congratulations! You get to live!

> *They whoop with joy.*

ROBERT: Your puny planet will be spared – from us. You guys are so cute. Of course, you'll destroy yourselves in time, but that's to be expected. I like that story.

TED: What do we do now?

ROBERT: Whatever you want.

INDIRA: We're still in this weird place.

ROBERT: Oh, right. Lie back down on those surfaces and when you wake up, you'll be back in your bed. Like none of this has happened. Like it's all a dream. Like in that movie you people love: The Wizard of Oz. "And you were there, and you were there."

ADAM: What do you mean "you people"?

> *Robert's confused.*

INDIRA: Will we remember that this happened?

ROBERT: Why wouldn't you remember?

ADAM: That's usually the way it works in the movies. Anyway, thanks.

> *Everyone goes back to their table. Lies down. Adam sits up and notices that Robert's still there.*

ROBERT: You're all so cute. (beat) Have nice lives.

> *A flash of light and he's gone. They sit up and look at each other.*

ADAM: That was kind of fucked up.

TED: But it went well. We did it!! See you guys around the - See you guys around.

INDIRA: I hope not to see you people again.

ADAM: Sweet.

> *They lie down. The tables glow. The room glows blue.*

> *Blackout.*

> *End of play.*

# What You Did

# What You Did

*A theatre lobby. An East Indian woman is very engaged in looking at her cell phone and texting. A black man crosses through the lobby. Stops.*

MAN: I liked your - thing -

WOMAN: Oh. Thanks. Yours too. Interesting.

MAN: Yeah? (beat) When people use that word - you know -

WOMAN: I don't mean it that way.

MAN: No?

WOMAN: I liked it.

MAN: Ok. You don't have to.

WOMAN: I know. Free country.

MAN: Yep.

*Beat. She goes back to texting.*

MAN: Your stuff's not online. You said in the -

WOMAN: Yeah. Wanted to get it out first. I said that too, in there.

MAN: It didn't make sense to me, though, really. I mean, the internet is free -

WOMAN: Which is exactly why - Who cares if it's on the internet? Everybody's there. All kinds of - shitty stuff.

MAN: So, you're waiting for distribution?

WOMAN: I like the festivals.

MAN: I do too, but -

WOMAN: They feel special to me.

# What You Did

MAN: Ok. I just –

WOMAN: Yes?

MAN: – don't think it's mutually exclusive.

WOMAN: It's not. Clearly. My choice. Free country.

MAN: Yeah, right, of course.

WOMAN: Yeah. (beat) Anything else?

MAN: Well, I – saw what you did in there.

WOMAN: Where? Inside? What'd I do?

MAN: No, in your piece. I saw what you did –

WOMAN: Meaning – comedy?

MAN: No, that's not what I – it was funny. You were good and I like your co-star a lot. Her work is always – I like her.

WOMAN: So what are you – ?

MAN: I'm just saying you – surrounded yourself with –

WOMAN: With –

MAN: White people.

WOMAN: Oh.

MAN: Yeah. I mean – I get it.

WOMAN: What do you get?

MAN: You know –

WOMAN: No –

MAN: Well that you're instantly more – "marketable" that way. That people will watch. More people. Instantly. Not that that's bad –

149

# What You Did

WOMAN: You think I engineered it that way?

MAN: Well, everything's a choice. Right? You're the only person of color in your own web series - that's like -

WOMAN: What?

MAN: It's like -

WOMAN: Yeah? What? Something bad, right? Something racist or -

MAN: No, you can't be racist. (beat) You know, because you can't reverse the power dynamic - It's not the same thing.

WOMAN: Are you lecturing me on racism now?

MAN: Clarifying.

WOMAN: Which you assume I don't know?

MAN: No, I'm just -

WOMAN: What?

MAN: Clarifying.

WOMAN: Ok. (beat) And you think I manipulated this whole thing.

MAN: I didn't say that.

WOMAN: You kinda did. You said - implied - that by - no you said that by being the only person of color in my web series - that I - what did you say?

MAN: I didn't actually finish my thought -

WOMAN: Gamed the system? What?

MAN: Well, yeah, kinda. I get it. I did say I get it.

WOMAN: You're such a presumptuous -

# What You Did

MAN: So, you didn't do that? You weren't the only person of color in your web series? Because unless those people were "colored" –

WOMAN: Nobody says that anymore.

MAN: I'm using in the broadest –

WOMAN: Oh my god.

MAN: Don't make this me – This isn't me – I'm not making this more than it is.

WOMAN: You are!

MAN: No, I'm stating what it is. That it is. That's what you did. That's who you cast and it's your project –

WOMAN: Unlike you who – had an all-black cast.

MAN: Not all black.

WOMAN: Mostly.

MAN: Yes.

WOMAN: So that makes you – what?

MAN: Nothing – just – more –

WOMAN: Yes?

MAN: Straightforward maybe. More realistic.

WOMAN: I happen to live in a world that looks like my series.

MAN: Oh yeah?

WOMAN: Yes!

MAN: Your DP, though. That guy you introduced. That Asian guy.

WOMAN: Oh my god.

# What You Did

MAN: I'm just saying. That's apparently not the world you live in if your DP was an Asian guy. You just didn't have any in your series. Which is -

WOMAN: Yes, what? What are you accusing me of?

MAN: Even the love interests. All those guys. (beat) It's at least - worth mentioning.

WOMAN: Is it?

MAN: I'm mentioning it.

WOMAN: Frankly, I don't give a shit what you think of that.

MAN: What do you think of it?

WOMAN: I think it's - what I chose to do.

MAN: And why?

WOMAN: Because I did?

MAN: You're saying, you didn't choose that to gain favor with the audience - to make your piece more producible.

WOMAN: I produced it myself. It was producible.

MAN: More producible.

WOMAN: The producibility was not in question.

MAN: Because you had so many white people in it.

WOMAN: What is it with you?

MAN: What is it with you? Look, I'm not casting aspersions -

WOMAN: Who uses that word -

MAN: I'm not throwing rocks at you. I'm saying I know what you did. And I'm not immune to the charms of white people and that status quo. And I get how it works - we all do. Because I grew up wanting to be them. Wishing I was in Full House or whatever. I know they draw a crowd. And how adorable they are with their ruddy faces and their blue eyes and their hair sticking straight up or flinged – flung? – to the side. I know how they're everywhere and how comforting and "normal" it seems to sit in the dark or at home or watch a play or whatever the fuck you do – and see them. I know how much they are the focus of 90% of everything. I love them, too. I love their straight noses and their adorable slightly nasal sweetness. I get all the flavors – the charming hipster we love to hate, and the silly stoner, and the surfer dude, and the slightly dim bear-ish guy who is probably into comic books, and the sweet young thing, the sexy blonde girl who is a tease. I get it – the universe is theirs and has been since the beginning of time. And I get, because I went to private school, how juicy it can be to be the only speck in a sea of vanilla. How it's an instant spotlight for you – the perfect way to lift yourself up – get people to notice. People who might not if you made some pseudo Bollywood shit. You've made a thing that people can say, "She's just like us." And that will get you noticed. While people like me – telling an authentic story –

WOMAN: Authentic?? Your piece is Science Fiction –

MAN: People like me are populating my work with diverse actors and in some way – just fading into the woodwork.

WOMAN: For god's sake –

MAN: While you ride the coattails of the Eurocentric actors to get their audience. (beat) That's it. That's all I'm saying. That I saw it. What you did.

WOMAN: You're a fucking moron.

MAN: Because I'm telling you the truth?

WOMAN: You're putting words – You just – vomited all over me – this racist –

MAN: Nuh uh –

WOMAN: Race-conscious bullshit projection –

MAN: That you can't deny.

WOMAN: I'm denying it. It's all you –

# What You Did

MAN: It's the world. You know it's true.

WOMAN: You can't tell me what I know.

MAN: Ok. If that's the way you want to play it.

WOMAN: I made a piece of art, and I can do whatever the fuck I want in it.

MAN: You sure curse a lot.

WOMAN: Fuck you.

MAN: And what makes me me – is I'm the kinda guy who points stuff out. So that's what I did. I know what you did. And I'm telling ya.

WOMAN: Uh huh.

MAN: You should thank me.

WOMAN: What?

MAN: For my honesty? For my straightforwardness. Clearly no one's had the balls to tell you –

WOMAN: I'm done. I'm done with you – I'm done with this conversation.

MAN: I had the balls. Just to say I see it.

>    *He starts out.*

WOMAN: Well, you spot it, you got it.

MAN: What do you mean by that?

WOMAN: If it bothers you. If you notice – then the reverse is true.

MAN: What reverse? What?

WOMAN: That if you noticed my piece had only one person of color: me. Then you also noticed that your piece was wall-to-wall black people.

# What You Did

MAN: Wall-to-wall?

WOMAN: With a few white people thrown in. So you were trying to say something too, especially since you went to private school and - Some of your best friends are white people.

MAN: I never said that.

WOMAN: You're not denying it. So you were making a statement - saying, I don't know - that you belong with black people. That you think, perhaps, it's more mainstream to create a sci-fi web series for the dark-skinned crowd? Maybe it's more marketable -

MAN: Oh please -

WOMAN: Since it looks like - all those 'black shows' and movies. You went ghetto.

MAN: Screw you! There's nothing ghetto about -

WOMAN: You're right. Your black people were so well-spoken. I see what you're doing there. Turning the norms on their heads.

MAN: What's not normal about that?

WOMAN: Well - compared to what the universal white man sees, you're really shaking it up for us - them. That's quite a revolution.

MAN: I made a choice.

WOMAN: Ah. Is that what you did?

> *Beat. An Asian guy comes up to the woman.*

GUY: Hey.

WOMAN: You ready?

> *He looks at the man. Beat.*

GUY: I'm Gerald.

MAN: Mike.

WOMAN: I'm ready.

GUY: Ok.

*They start out. A white man comes in, very attractive.*

WHITE MAN: Honey, I've been waiting.

*The woman looks at this and nods at the man.*

MAN: Sorry. I got – sorry.

*The white man clocks the woman. And looks at the man: Is everything alright? The woman leans in.*

WOMAN: Nice talking to you.

MAN: Yeah.

WOMAN: I see what you did.

*She turns on her heels and exits.*

WHITE MAN: What did you do?

*Blackout.*

# IDENTITY

*"Art is a lie that tells the truth."*

*-Pablo Picasso*

# Give Me the Card

*A black man walks into the space, nervous and confused. He's dressed in an upscale casual outfit. He calls out.*

MAN: Hello? Is anyone here?

*A spotlight comes on, blinds the man for a moment. His eyes adjust. The urban voice of a black woman is heard.*

VOICE: Yeah. He'll be right back with you. Hang on.

MAN: Ok, but I don't quite know how this works.

VOICE: What's your name?

MAN: Richard –

VOICE: Never mind, I found you, honey. Stand by.

MAN: Ok.

*He fidgets. MUSIC plays – Something funky, soulful, black (Stevie Wonder's Ngiculela – Es Una Historia – I Am Singing for example). The man is startled at first. Looks at his watch, annoyed. Then – a noise from somewhere off. The man squints – makes out someone. The music stops.*

MAN: Hi! Mr. Um – is that you?

*He waves.*

VOICE: It's him.

*Mr. Black has a booming voice. James Earl Jones on steroids.*

MR. BLACK: Yeah, have a seat.

*The man looks around. No chair.*

MAN: Where?

MR. BLACK: The floor's too good for you?

MAN: No - not. But, I'll stand, thanks.

MR. BLACK: Figures. We need your card.

MAN: I'm sorry?

MR. BLACK: Your card. Your African-American, black person, Negro, Colored people membership card. We need it back.

MAN: Why?

MR. BLACK: You know why.

MAN: I - don't. Did you issue a new design or something?

MR. BLACK: *You're not really black.*

MAN: What?

MR. BLACK: Turn your card in.

MAN: I don't understand.

MR. BLACK: So, you dumb now?

MAN: You're not making any sense!

MR. BLACK: You hate hip-hop.

MAN: And -

MR. BLACK: You don't like basketball.

MAN: I'm not a sports guy.

MR. BLACK: You like hot sauce?

MAN: No.

MR. BLACK: Exactly.

MAN: And that means I have to -

MR. BLACK: Turn it in. We don't have all day.

MAN: This doesn't make any sense.

MR. BLACK: You don't like watermelon. Black-eyed peas. Fried chicken.

MAN: I like fried chicken!

MR. BLACK: You eat it, but you think it's greasy and bad for you. You won't have it with waffles and you always hate yourself after.

MAN: It gives me a stomach ache.

MR. BLACK: Genetically, that's not right.

MAN: That's biology. That's digestion.

MR. BLACK: It's abnormal.

MAN: That's not a reasonable –

MR. BLACK: And you can't dance.

MAN: I dance!

MR. BLACK: You *think* you can dance.

MAN: I won a dance contest once.

MR. BLACK: Third grade.

MAN: So?

MR. BLACK: Plus, you were raised Catholic.

MAN: But – you knew all this before. It's the 21st century –

MR. BLACK: We just voted.

MAN: We? You had a meeting? I didn't get an invite.

MR. BLACK: It's over. We got rules. It's done.

MAN: No. I should have been there. Isn't there a loophole? Some other way? Come on! Please.

> *Beat. The sound of Mr. Black covering his mic. He's talking this over with someone.*

MR. BLACK: Alright.

> *The man brightens.*

MR. BLACK: Speed round.

MAN: What? I thought I would just get to keep it.

> *A loud TICKING SOUND starts.*

MR. BLACK: Who won The Soul Train Music Awards this year?

MAN: Lots of people.

MR. BLACK: Name ONE.

MAN: Beyonce?

> *DING! He's right! He's surprised.*

MR. BLACK: Name three shows on BET.

MAN: Uh – The Soul Train Music Awards. And... The Tyler Perry Show?

> *BUZZZZZ! Wrong.*

MR. BLACK: What's Oprah's middle name?

MAN: Minerva?

> *BUZZZZZ! Wrong.*

MR. BLACK: Obama's shoe size?

> *The man opens his mouth to speak. He has no idea. The clock runs out. A final BUZZER sounds.*

# Give Me the Card

MR. BLACK: Pathetic.

MAN: Wait. I'm black.

MR. BLACK: Not anymore.

MAN: You don't get to decide this. Look at me! I've been stared at by white folks. Followed in 7-11! When I see a police car, I break out in hives. I've been called the "N" word. I saw Black Panther five times! Wakanda Forever! I have a larger than average penis!

MR. BLACK: You *think* you do. (beat) We're building our power as a people.

MAN: Without me?

MR. BLACK: Gotta cut the dead weight.

> *Beat.*

MAN: What am I supposed to put on government applications?

MR. BLACK: "Other". Hand over the card. Or we'll take it.

> *The sound of footsteps: a small army advancing. Panicked, the man pulls out his wallet, devastated. Opens it. Takes out his card. Stares at it.*

MAN: No, it's my card!! I'm black!

> *He runs, dodging the spotlight. It tries to follow him. He's gone. Beat.*

VOICE: Damn!

MR. BLACK: He was fast. Alright people – we got another one on the loose. You know what to do!

> *Sirens blare.*

> *Blackout.*

# How to Teach the Civil War

*Lights up on Shana, black, 14, smart with a combative side. She wears the outfit of a confederate soldier. Bombs can be heard going off in the background. The stage is dark.*

SHANA: I'm dodging bullets as I run through the field. Muskets being fired around me. I can't see shit – it's raining dust and mud. I'm jumping as I run – over bodies I'm too scared to look down and identify. I don't wanna know. Just wanna make it to safety, outta this. In my mind I see the fireplace at home and Buster curled up on the rug asleep. I'm gonna make it. I told them I would and I will.

ELLIS: Shana!

*Lights shift. We're in a well-appointed living room. It's messy – there are books and pillows, a backpack, shoes not put away, mail on a chair. Shana is seated on the couch, a video game controller in her hands. She snakes and moves – engrossed in the game. Ellis, 40s, black, upscale and well spoken, stands next to her. She doesn't notice.*

ELLIS: Shana!

*Ellis snatches the controller from her. She snaps to – shocked to see him standing there, "bullying" her.*

SHANA: I was playing.

ELLIS: I was calling you.

SHANA: What?

ELLIS: I asked you to clean your room.

SHANA: 'sclean.

ELLIS: And to take that (The uniform.) off.

SHANA: I'm getting into character.

ELLIS: Off!

*She shakes her head and walks out. She's had it. The explosions continue.*

ELLIS: You're returning it tomorrow.

SHANA: I need it for class.

ELLIS: You heard me!

*Ellis sighs. He glances at his watch and starts picking up things around the room. Shana comes back in wearing a T-shirt and jeans - costume free. Beat.*

SHANA: Who's coming over?

ELLIS: Turn that off (The video game.). (beat. Of the cleaning.) You can help.

*She helps.*

SHANA: You're acting weird. (beat) We having company?

ELLIS: Yes.

*The doorbell rings. Ellis looks at Shana. The living room is still not clean. He stacks a huge pile of stuff: books, newspapers, mail, some clothing, shoes. Shana watches, bewildered. Ellis scampers out of the room. The doorbell rings again. Shana grabs a stack of magazines from a neat pile in the corner and drops them on the floor, as Ellis re-enters. He can't believe she's made a new mess in the time he was out of the room.*

SHANA: Sorry.

*Beat. She knows she's in the wrong - starts to pick up the magazines. He gets the door. Smith, 40s, white, very buttoned up, stands there holding a plate of cookies. Shana's surprised to see him.*

SHANA: Hi!

SMITH: Hi Shana. Ellis. (beat) Nice place.

*Ellis lets him in.*

ELLIS: What's that?

SMITH: Cookies. Linda made 'em. Chocolate chip with – other stuff. Nuts I think. (beat) Sorry we missed the house warming.

*He holds them out to Ellis. Beat. Ellis takes the plate. There's an awkward vibe between these two.*

ELLIS: You didn't have to bring cookies.

SMITH: I wanted to. You made it sound serious. Linda was worried. So – cookies.

*Smith's cell phone rings. Something classical.*

SMITH: Linda. (beat) Hi honey. I'm here.

ELLIS: Hi Linda. I'm Fine!

SHANA: Hi!

SMITH: I'll let you know.

SHANA: Dad – I don't think you have the right –

ELLIS: Excuse me?

*Smith hangs up.*

SMITH: The right to what?

ELLIS: This Civil War thing –

SMITH: I knew it.

ELLIS: I don't think you should be teaching it this way.

SMITH: You don't like my lesson plan. (beat) It's experiential, Ellis. That's the way kids learn.

SHANA: He doesn't want me in it.

# How to Teach the Civil War

ELLIS: I don't even get it –

SMITH: That's my point. You have to *do* it to get it.

ELLIS: You're going to have them running around with fake weapons pretending to die all over the lacrosse field.

SMITH: Schools are doing this all over the country.

ELLIS: She's a Confederate soldier.

SMITH: You're too sensitive.

ELLIS: My daughter is wearing the uniform of the people who enslaved her ancestors and you think the issue is I'm too sensitive? How many other black kids are pledging allegiance to Dixie?

SMITH: Six.

SHANA: Six.

> *Beat.*

SHANA: It was my choice.

> *Ellis turns to her, dumbfounded.*

SHANA: I thought it would be – like a lesson in empathy.

ELLIS: Empathy for slaveholders? You don't know what you're talking about.

SHANA: I know what happened. I'm not dumb. I made a choice.

ELLIS: The wrong choice.

SHANA: I thought I'd push myself.

SHANA: Don't beat up on him – he's a good teacher! Mostly.

SMITH: The kids are excited about – What do you mean mostly?

SHANA: Too much homework.

ELLIS: Stop! We are not doing a review of your teaching.

SHANA: Yeah you were.

SMITH: It sounded like -

ELLIS: I am, yes! Not you. Go! Go - read or something.

SHANA: It's about me. I'm not leaving.

ELLIS: Then be quiet. (beat) The confederate thing is ridiculous.

SMITH: It's educational.

ELLIS: It's fantasy. And you're allowing it. You're taking a piece of history and you're making into - a Disneyland attraction: "Civil War Land". It's not that - it's - I get that you want to teach these kids how it was - but then I say teach them how it was. Let the white kids - the boys be the soldiers, have the white girls sit out -

SMITH: You want some of them to be slaves?

ELLIS: Of course!

SHANA: There were black troops, Dad. Didn't you see 'Glory'?

ELLIS: Fine. Then do that. But don't mix them. The black boys can fight - separately for the Union side. All the girls can stay behind.

SMITH: Some blacks fought for the Confederacy.

ELLIS: They did?

SHANA: See!

ELLIS: Well you're not doing it. (beat) They were forced to participate that way. Must have been. I'm not letting you do it.

SMITH: Everyone in my class wants to be involved.

ELLIS: That's not what the Civil War is - was. It was about division and separation. Let it be about that. Let that be the lesson. (beat) I can't be the only parent to complain about this.

SMITH: No.

ELLIS: Right.

SMITH: You're the only person to complain about it. (beat) When you get a Masters in Education –

ELLIS: I don't need a Masters. Shana's not participating in this.

SHANA: You can't do that!

ELLIS: Done! (To Smith.) And you're going to cancel this exercise.

SMITH: No I'm not.

ELLIS: Or I'm calling the principal tomorrow.

>   *Beat.*

SMITH: You won't do that.

ELLIS: We'll see what he thinks.

SMITH: It's my classroom.

ELLIS: It's my daughter.

SMITH: She's out! You said. She'll get an incomplete.

SHANA: No! That's not fair. (beat) I'm right here! Don't talk like I'm not here. You can't both act like – whatever – because you feel like it. I'm not your slave.

ELLIS: Go!

SHANA: Your idea of the exercise sounds boring anyway. No one would want to do that.

ELLIS: It's history!

SMITH: It's middle school!

# How to Teach the Civil War

ELLIS: You want them to fight with each other - or pretend? Like in those video games - all explosions all the time. You're contributing to the dumbing down of America.

SMITH: Oh, right, I've done your people wrong.

ELLIS: My people? Which people?

SMITH: I don't know - gay, black, single parents, architects. Which one are you today? You're still so angry, you've been saying this crap since college.

ELLIS: I was excited she was going to be in your class. But you can't whitewash the Civil War. Much as you'd like to. It's wrong.

*Beat.*

SHANA: It's an exercise. It's just - it was gonna be fun. I already know about the war anyway: not all black women sat around - Harriet Tubman was a spy! I already know about it. I do my own research - about everything. I already know.

ELLIS: But you didn't fight to change it. You fight me all the time.

*Beat. She shrugs.*

SMITH: I'll pray on it.

ELLIS: Spoken like a Mormon.

*Smith grabs a pillow and throws it at Ellis. Ellis catches it.*

SMITH: I'll admit I - prefer teaching the Civil War this way. It feels right to me. I'm comfortable with it. It simplifies things, so what. If kids want to know more - they can find out more. (beat) Call the office, fine. Complain if you think that's the right way to go. (beat) See you tomorrow, Shana.

SHANA: I apologize for my dad.

ELLIS: Hey!

SHANA: I do. (beat) Take your cookies. We don't deserve them.

*She walks over to him, but instead of grabbing the cookies, she hugs him. Then she straightens up, grabs the plate and hands it to him - business like.*

SHANA: Keep thinking outside the box.

*She smacks him on the arm like a football coach.*

SMITH: Thanks. I won't give you an incomplete. We'll figure something out.

*He puts the cookies down someplace else and goes. Beat. Shana stares at Ellis.*

SHANA: I thought it would be fun. Dodging bullets. Pretending to defend myself. It'd be just like laser tag.

*She goes. Ellis grabs the pillow from the floor and puts it on the couch. He sits. Sighs big. He grabs a remote from the couch and turns on the TV. Then grabs the video game controller. Presses a button. We hear some electronic sounds as Ellis selects something.*

*Introductory music sounds - then an explosion. Ellis starts playing, swaying side to side as he does - locked in battle as the lights fade.*

*End of play.*

# Part of This is True?

# Part of This is True?

*Tom, 30s, black, upscale, is standing with Rhetta, 30s, black, outside a building. There's a stage door near them. Spotlight on Tom. He turns to us.*

TOM: (To us.) With things the way they are in the world, I sometimes don't know where reality and imagination meet. So I'm not sure which part of this is true and which part isn't.

*Lights shift.*

TOM: I'm glad you came with me tonight.

RHETTA: Me, too. It's good to hear the perspective on things. How it works in the industry and why they make stupid stuff.

TOM: He didn't admit the shows were stupid.

RHETTA: He's not going to do that. He's the head of the studio. He's got to defend it all. Corporate speak. All that. (beat) TV is crap.

TOM: There's some good stuff.

RHETTA: Keep telling yourself that. You think he'll remember you?

*Lights shift. Tom talks to us again.*

TOM: (To us.) I don't know what anyone remembers. Used to feel like I was invisible. The black guy in the corner. But today? We're all pretty vivid. Or we have the power to be. At least in theory.

*Lights shift.*

RHETTA: What are you going to say to him?

TOM: I don't know.

RHETTA: I want to watch - whatever you're doing. To learn. (beat) I would love your career. You know that.

TOM: You hate TV.

RHETTA: I love money.

## Part of This is True?

*Lights shift.*

TOM: (To us.) My parents taught me the rules of talking to white people. A way to be that's been passed down for centuries. I'm good with rules.

> *Lights shift. The stage door opens. A Bodyguard – all muscle, sunglasses and bravado steps out. And then Huck, 40s, white, corporate, moneyed without trying to seem to be, emerges and looks around. Flashes a polite smile to Tom and Rhetta.*

RHETTA: I liked your talk.

HUCK: Thank you. (To the guard.) Where's the car?

BODYGUARD: Coming around.

HUCK: Then why did we come out here?

TOM: I thought it was interesting, your take on programming. I mean, you said you want to engage families.

HUCK: We do. That's the mandate.

TOM: But your stuff is so violent. I mean – it features violence. Front and center, you know?

HUCK: Many of our programs don't.

TOM: Two of them: "August March" and that hospital one.

RHETTA: "Collingwood" –

TOM: Yeah. Those are tame but the rest –

HUCK: Keep watching. I think you'll be surprised.

TOM: I doubt it.

> *Huck reacts. Lights shift.*

TOM: (To us.) My heart is pounding. Because I don't do this normally. Ever. Is this even real? (beat. To Huck.) You remember me?

# Part of This is True?

HUCK: We've never met.

*Lights shift.*

TOM: (To us.) "The Spook that sat by the door." "The Negro in the corner."

*Lights shift.*

TOM: Williamstown. I was an intern. Out of college.

HUCK: I don't - sorry.

TOM: About 20 years ago?

HUCK: Doesn't ring a bell.

*Lights shift.*

TOM: (To us.) I rang some bells back then.

*Lights shift.*

TOM: We had sex.

HUCK: What?

TOM: Yeah, you were still drinking. According to your book.

*Lights shift.*

TOM: (To us.) My heart's about to leap out of my chest. That dude might actually take me out. Breathe!

*Lights shift.*

HUCK: Oh my god. Did I - I totally - I'm sorry.

TOM: Don't be. We had a really good -

HUCK: And this is your -

TOM: My wife. Kidding. Friend. She knows all about it.

RHETTA: Maybe not *all* about it.

HUCK: Well. I'm embarrassed.

*Lights shift.*

TOM: (To us.) I like him embarrassed. Is that wrong?

*Lights shift.*

RHETTA: He's very successful now. He's a writer. For TV and comic books.

TOM: I write futuristic science fiction dramas about race. (To us.) He's about to ask me what shows I've written for.

HUCK: Congratulations. (beat) Any word about the car?

BODYGUARD: Still coming. Traffic, sorry.

HUCK: Maybe we should wait inside.

TOM: (To us.) Or not. What am I doing wrong? If I'm going do this, I need this shit to work. (To Huck.) Maybe I wasn't the only intern you slept with? Maybe the only black one?

HUCK: It was a long time ago. I wasn't very – present then – with the drinking, I mean.

TOM: You're different now, huh? (To us.) I want to see him groveling. Begging to know my work. I want him to say:

HUCK: You know, you should send me some material. I'd like to – have my people read you.

TOM: (To us.) And then I would say. (To Huck.) No, you wouldn't. You've asked me before. When I was in playwriting school – you weren't yet – famous. 12 years ago, maybe – I introduced myself – again and – You had come to speak at the school –

RHETTA: He went to Yale.

TOM: – about the industry and you said I could leave you a play to read, that you'd be interested in reading it. And I left that play at the reception desk. Which you asked me to do. In an envelope with your name on it.

HUCK: And –

TOM: You didn't pick it up. You left without it. Guess you weren't interested really. *You fucking shallow piece of* –

*Lights shift.*

TOM: (To us.) But he doesn't say that. He doesn't ask for anything. He doesn't care about me. My ideas, my creativity. My black / queer soul. It makes no difference to him.

*Lights shift.*

HUCK: Williamstown was a long time ago. I wasn't very – present then – with the drinking, I mean.

TOM: You're different now, huh?

HUCK: Yes. I am.

TOM: Really? Or is that just something you say? Earlier you said "I'd be surprised" – about your programming. But I'm not surprised by you. You're all about what you're all about. And there's no – penetrating that. Even though way back then you didn't have a problem with –

HUCK: You don't know me.

TOM: (To us.) And he says that, and something clicks in my head. A little voice whispers: *Maybe he's right. Maybe you don't know him at all. He could be a sweet guy who is trying really hard to reconcile his privilege and whiteness and attempting to be kind in this moment with me – even as I attack him. Maybe he's got a black, or Asian, or Latino husband who he loves more than anything. And he's done his race work and reads Robin DiAngelo and Ta-Nehisi Coates.* And I hear him say:

HUCK: I'm sorry if we had a misunderstanding. I'm sorry.

TOM: (To us.) And what if he is sorry? And I've misjudged him. Even though he didn't remember me and left my script behind when he had the chance to read it. What if I'm risking my professional reputation just by saying these exact things in public space? Like I'm setting myself up for a professional lynching just by speaking my mind. Why am I no longer following the rules? My heart rate slows. And I notice he's kinda cute. This older version of him is sort of adorable.

*Lights shift.*

HUCK: I'm sorry if we had a misunderstanding. I'm sorry.

TOM: Thanks for that. For being sorry.

*A moment passes.*

HUCK: Nice seeing you again.

*Huck puts out his hand to shake. Tom looks at his hand.*

TOM: On your network – there are barely any people of color. We were talking about this the other day.

RHETTA: We were.

HUCK: Our intention is –

TOM: To diversify? You said that in your talk. But I don't think you want to change the system or you would have done it. All the stuff you're doing works so well for you. White guys built this system. Why would you want it to change?

BODYGUARD: Hold on –

HUCK: It's fine.

TOM: Is it? You aired that animated show last year.

RHETTA: "Gernomimo Falls".

TOM: Nice Indian name. Indian characters – all white voices.

BODYGUARD: Let's go back inside.

# Part of This is True?

HUCK: No. You're right about that. I don't have any excuses. These are the things we're talking about every day. Looking for solutions. Trying to figure out what the next steps are. This is not easy for me. For any of us who – I'm questioning everything I've been taught. I'm re-examining all of my pre-conceptions. I'm in therapy. Consciousness groups. I want to do better. (beat) What would you like to see on TV?

TOM: My own show.

*Huck starts laughing. Tom is deadly serious.*

HUCK: I can't do that.

TOM: You don't even know what my show is about. (beat) Look, at least hire some black writers and black actors and other people of color, more women. I'd like see the corporate face of your studio change.

HUCK: I'm just one guy.

*Lights shift.*

TOM: (To us.) And again, the voice whispers that I might have him wrong. That maybe he is doing his best and it's an uphill battle. That maybe I shouldn't hold him responsible for all this shit that's been going on. That maybe the rules are worth paying attention to, and that my polite Negro self is a better weapon than ever opening my mouth and saying anything. What have I done? What have I said?

*Lights shift. A strobe light flashes – the scene is rewinding.*

HUCK: Nice seeing you again.

*Huck puts out his hand to shake. Tom shakes his hand.*

TOM: I understand that you think you've really done stuff. But, just so you know, I don't need a band-aid. I need real change. (beat) Please. My professional life, my well being depends on it. I really hope you get the relevance of all this. That your people owned my people and that what's happening in the media is continued subjugation. And that you people have NEVER apologized and I still feel the weight of your superiority on my back. Back in slave days, like now, your people were not all that interested in my people. Except to make a buck. They– wanted what they wanted. That's America. (beat. To us.) But I don't say any of that. Not one word.

> *Lights shift. The scene rewinds. Huck and the Bodyguard go back through the stage door.*

RHETTA: I want to watch - whatever you're doing. To learn. (beat) I would love your career. You know that.

TOM: You hate TV.

RHETTA: I love money.

> *Huck and the Bodyguard come out of the door.*

RHETTA: I liked your talk.

HUCK: Thank you.

BODYGUARD: The car is coming down the block.

TOM: I thought it was interesting, your take on programming. I mean, you said you want to engage families.

HUCK: We do. That's the mandate.

TOM: Well, I hope it happens. I'm Tom. We - met at Williamstown.

HUCK: Oh. I don't recall.

> *Tom stares at Huck, calculating his response.*

TOM: That's ok. Congratulations on all your success.

> *Huck stares at Tom for a long moment.*

HUCK: Thanks.

> *Huck and the Bodyguard go.*

RHETTA: I though you were - You had a whole thing to say to him.

> *Tom looks at Rhetta. Then at us.*

183

TOM: Yeah. I thought I did, too. (beat) But I guess – I don't know – Didn't seem like the right time.

RHETTA: You ok?

TOM: I don't know.

*End of play.*

section six

# RELATIONSHIPS

*"Kindness eases change, love quiets fear."*

*-Octavia Butler, Parable of the Sower*

# Things Are (mostly) Crazy

# Things Are (mostly) Crazy

*Lights up on a bench in Jackson Square Park.*

*Aaron, an Asian man in his 20s, is sitting reading a NYC guidebook. There is a single-use camera in his lap. Kurt, 30s and black enters, wearing a suit and looking around. He seems a bit rushed. He and Aaron catch eyes. A moment.*

AARON: Mostly I get it - the numbered streets. But the village I mostly don't get.

KURT: It's confusing.

AARON: Christopher Street?

KURT: About 8 blocks - that way.

AARON: OK. I figured. 8 blocks.

KURT: Down there.

AARON: I wanna see everything. But I'm like that mostly.

KURT: Good luck.

> *Kurt sits. Looks at his watch. Looks at Aaron who's still looking. They smile.*

KURT: What have you seen?

AARON: Empire State. Central Park. MOMA. I'm basically too excited to remember it all. So I mostly take pictures. (He snaps one of Kurt.) I'll send it to you.

BOXER: You're not his type.

> *Boxer suddenly appears. He's in his 40s, tall, bear-ish, intense. Lots of bluster, but ultimately unsteady and vulnerable.*

AARON: How do you know?

BOXER: I'm his type.

# Things Are (mostly) Crazy

KURT: Hey!

BOXER: You know I speak the truth. (Turning to Aaron.) See ya.

KURT: That's rude. Why are you being like this?

BOXER: Truthful? You know I'm right.

KURT: This is why I stay away.

*Aaron shoots a picture of Boxer. Boxer turns. Aaron runs.*

KURT: Prick. (beat) I don't like it when you act like that. (beat) Don't get quiet now. You can't pull that. That kid - is - a kid - and he's a tourist. I won't hang out with you if you don't act right.

BOXER: What does that mean?

KURT: You have to be nice.

BOXER: I don't feel nice - feel well.

KURT: You taking your pills? (beat) Boxer - are you taking -

BOXER: Yes. Yes. (beat) I'm taking them. (beat) I just see these people with you and I get -

KURT: Keep it to yourself. We're not -

BOXER: I know. (beat) Miss me?

KURT: Why don't you feel well?

BOXER: It's just general.

KURT: So - basically you're fine? You're not fine?

BOXER: I'm good now. (beat) Lauren - wants me to move - to be near her.

KURT: I thought you hated Montreal.

BOXER: I know. Yeah. (beat) So I'm gonna go.

KURT: Just because your sister asked you?

BOXER: I'm in a rut.

KURT: Did you talk to - your - group?

BOXER: I can make a decision, Kurt. Don't act like I can't.

KURT: So - when do you go?

BOXER: Soon. (beat) Why do you care? (beat) You want to get back together?

KURT: You're moving. What are we talking about? Box - I don't have this much time - I have to eat and get back -

BOXER: Yeah. And I'm moving - so. See ya. (beat)

KURT: Wanna go to lunch?

BOXER: No. No. You're busy. I'm busy. I just wanted to tell you. (beat) I'm a different guy now. I take the stuff. I'm different. And - it was a hypothetical - the getting together.

KURT: Yeah. Ok. (beat) I'm not seeing anyone - so - that's not it. But I don't think it would be good for us. Me. Sorry. (beat) Aren't you hungry? (Boxer shakes his head.) How's Lauren?

BOXER: Good. She asks about you.

KURT: Tell her hi.

BOXER: She'll want more than that.

KURT: Tell her New York is still as strange - stranger than ever. Crazy. Tell her - I still take ballroom dance sometimes and I have a new Chinese place I like to go to on weekends.

BOXER: Where?

KURT: Never mind. Tell her to take good care of you - or else. (beat) I could find some violation - issue a subpoena.

BOXER: I've seen your subpoena.

> *They laugh. It gets awkward. Boxer pulls out a photo, shows it*
> *to Kurt.*

KURT: Oh god! Where did you find that?

BOXER: Found it. Provincetown.

KURT: I know. Jeff. We never should have gone on vacation with him.

BOXER: Talk about needy.

KURT: It's today, isn't it?

BOXER: Three years. I went to church. Lit a candle.

KURT: Good. What a diva!

BOXER: Diva bitch. He knew I was crazy before I knew.

KURT: You're not crazy.

BOXER: Was. (beat) Was. (beat) I washed my hair today. You used to
do it. You'd play with it too - run your hands through. Feel it.

KURT: No. I don't know what I want now. Therapy has been all about
that.

BOXER: Ok. Seen any movies?

KURT: No. I've been working late. Or sleeping.

BOXER: You depressed?

KURT: No. (beat) You seen any?

BOXER: A few things. Old stuff. 'Big' 'Gods & Monsters', 'Tootsie',
'Serpico', 'Frances', 'Vertigo.' Not many.

KURT: Sounds like a lot.

BOXER: It's not. (beat) Ok. (beat) So there's this girl – in my group. She's new. I swear she's flirting with me the first day. And I'm thinking – You know how I get – nervous – that I'm responsible somehow or something. And I'm thinking 'I could wait until something comes up and then tell her.' But I don't want to wait either – so I just tell her. "I'm gay!" No revving up – just like that. And she just stares at me. (He imitates her look.) She's cool with it now. And I'm not nervous.

KURT: I finally put that picture of Bill Pullman up in my office. He helps me get through the day. And I'm mostly out – you know. But some of the new legal assistants – and we had clients in – these white women from Germany – they kind of looked twice.

BOXER: They'll get used to it. (beat) Whacking it much?

KURT: I'm not answering that.

BOXER: I am. You don't have to tell me. But you've got to clean out the system.

KURT: Can we not talk about sex?

BOXER: You used to like it.

KURT: When are you leaving?

BOXER: You getting rid of me? (beat) Tuesday.

KURT: That's soon. And Lauren and Rich are coming?

BOXER: I can travel by myself.

KURT: What about your stuff? Do you need help? Packing can be depressing.

BOXER: You think I don't know that? You don't have to tell me. You think you're being helpful?

KURT: I don't know what I think. I think I'm going to lunch. Call me before you go. If you want.

> *Aaron is suddenly there.*

AARON: I'm Aaron. Meant to ask your name.

KURT: Kurt.

AARON: I wanted to give you my card. So, if you're ever out west.

*Aaron holds out the card. Boxer stares at Kurt.*

KURT: I won't call you. I'm - taken. Not him.

AARON: You sure?

BOXER: He didn't stutter.

KURT: I am. Thanks, really.

AARON: OK. Back to the sights. Whatevs.

*Aaron waves and is gone.*

BOXER: Taken?

KURT: For him I am.

*Kurt sits. Boxer touches Kurt's hair.*

KURT: Stop. Don't - (beat) What did the library say? When you told them you were leaving.

BOXER: Good luck!

KURT: I bet they'll miss you. They'll miss your ugly plaid shirts. And you - going off your medication and then taking it.

BOXER: I don't do that!

KURT: Good. You used to. (beat) Last two weeks - I've been working these insane hours. I get in at 8 and leave around 11. I didn't want to be one of those people - there all the time - trying to do something that can only be accomplished on little sleep and extra caffeine. I'm one of those people now looking for my reward. It's sad. The real me's been replaced. Like 'Invasion of The Body Snatchers'.

BOXER: The original or the remake?

KURT: I'm going on meds.

BOXER: Are you?

KURT: Yeah. I haven't been feeling - you know.

BOXER: Yeah. But - it's alright.

KURT: I was - thinking - with the meds - maybe you could coach me through it.

BOXER: Always liked coaching you. (beat) Sure. I could.

KURT: I'll miss you, Box. I know there's the phone. I've been meaning to see you but with work and how I've been feeling -

BOXER: I'm not leaving. I made that up. I thought you'd beg me not to go -

KURT: That's so stupid.

BOXER: I've got - mental issues. (beat) I miss you, too.

KURT: You can't be like that. That's mean.

BOXER: I'll still tell Lauren you said hi. I'm sorry.

KURT: My mother still asks about you. I wish she wouldn't, but you know her. (beat) Want to go to the movies?

BOXER: You have to work. You're busy.

KURT: I could call in. Take the rest of the day.

BOXER: You could. You won't.

> *Kurt pulls out his cell. He speed dials.*

KURT: Henry - what do I have the rest of today? (beat) Uh - huh. Call him and cancel. I'm not feeling great - (beat) No - I'll be fine. I'll be back tomorrow. (beat) OK. (He hangs up.) Look at that. I called in. You were wrong.

BOXER: For once. What do you want to see?

KURT: Something upbeat. Or funny.

BOXER: You're buying lunch first, right?

KURT: Yeah. (beat) I guess I am.

*They lean into each other, playfully.*

*The lights fade.*

# Abstract Purple

PROLOGUE

*Lights up on Rosa. She wears a jean jacket, a purple T-shirt and jeans. She is running.*

ROSA: In the dream I'm running down some endless, dark street. I'm sweaty and tired. So tired. But I can't stop. I'm being chased by something big. If I stop, I will be eaten, chewed into little bloody pieces. My legs ache. I want to rest so badly, just to sit and relax. But I can't. Not now. Not ever. The thing is getting closer and I'm slowing down. I just can't run fast enough. I just can't. I trip. I fall. My face is wet. Am I crying? Or bleeding? I feel it hover over me. I hear it breathe. And then the pain - as claws slice through my clothes and into my skin and there's blood. So much blood. (beat) That's when I wake up. (beat) And I'm relieved. (beat) In reality I don't have to run. No one is chasing me. No one will. They don't care that much. They really don't see me. They see what they want to see: accomplishments, grades, report cards. They can't see me - how much I'm drowning in all the bullshit. (beat) I did this science project once: on ants - in an ant farm. Made a journal of their progress - studied them every day - took photographs. I HATE ants. All those legs, mandibles, antennae. But I kept them for six months. And fed them and wrote about them and watched them and used them. And hated them. (beat) I treated them like you treated me. So, I left. You'll miss me. You'll hurt. You'll be sorry - so sorry.

*Lights.*

SCENE ONE

*A well kept one room apartment. Against the back wall there is a small kitchenette with an L shaped counter defining the kitchen space. There's a radio on the counter. Downstage of the door is a dining table with two chairs. A convertible couch sits in the center of the room. On the left wall is a picture window. A hallway leading to the front door can be seen down right. Moonlight streams in through the window, casting everything in blue.*

*On the couch there are three painted canvasses side by side. They are abstract paintings, and they are the brightest and most colorful items in the apartment.*

*There's a knock at the door. Beat. Another knock. Beat. The sound of a lock being picked. The door opens quickly as Rosa sneaks in the apartment. There's a bright orange backpack slung over her shoulder. She grips her lower right arm in pain: she's bleeding. She shuts the door, moving cautiously. She's immediately startled by the sound of voices, until she realizes the radio is on.*

ROSA: Shit. Someone lives here.

*She turns toward the door when she hears a noise from the hallway. She steps away from the door. Beat. There's a key in the door.*

ROSA: Shit.

*Rosa ducks to one side of the counter as the front door opens. Mary walks in. She flips a light switch by the door. Mary is wearing a simple house dress and a light jacket. The colors are muted. She looks exhausted. Mary shuffles in slowly, carrying a grocery bag. She heads toward the couch – and seeing it's occupied with paintings, she crosses to the kitchen. She puts down her grocery bag. Outside, she hears police sirens.*

MARY: Ah, Joseph, give me strength. Police always chasing somebody.

*Beat. Mary hums a tune. Stops, clearly not remembering. She starts again. Stops. Shrugs. She takes her coat off, pulls a LIFE magazine from her bag, grabs her pocketbook and heads to the couch. She clears the paintings from the couch and sits. She holds the magazine so close it's almost touching her face. Even so she squints. Beat. She tosses the magazine aside in disgust.*

NEWSCASTER: This is W-I-N-S. Today's lottery numbers will be announced after these messages.

*Mary pulls a lottery ticket from her pocketbook. She kisses it and clenches it in her fist. Beat. She rises and heads to the bathroom. She enters and closes the door. Beat. The closet door opens and Rosa steps out. She starts for the door, stops and goes to the kitchen instead. She grabs an apple from the grocery bag and heads for the door. Mary re-enters. She gasps at seeing Rosa. They stare at each other.*

MARY: Hey - how'd you get in here?

*Rosa heads for the door.*

MARY: Hey - I asked you a question. How'd you get in?

ROSA: Flimsy locks? I've only been here a few minutes and - I'm sorry
- I -

MARY: I'm calling the police.

ROSA: Don't.

*Rosa pulls out a knife.*

MARY: Lord -

ROSA: Hey listen, Grandma, I'm leaving. I only took this apple -

MARY: What else you want?

ROSA: Nothing.

*Rosa heads toward the door.*

MARY: You're bleeding -

*Beat.*

MARY: You ain't gonna get far bleeding like that. Chances are you'll
leave a trail. That wouldn't be too clean a getaway.

ROSA: Don't worry about it.

MARY: I can't kid myself into thinking you ain't been here when you
here. How'm I gonna sleep thinking you out there bleeding to death?

ROSA: What are you - a retired comedian or something?

MARY: You came here for something - might have been a band-aid.

ROSA: It wasn't a band-aid, ok. I don't need one.

MARY: You're bleeding.

ROSA: I know!

MARY: Just trying to make sure you –

ROSA: Shut up!

*Beat.*

NEWSCASTER: Here are today's lottery numbers – get out your cards.

*Mary pulls out her card and looks at it.*

NEWSCASTER: Ready? 7, 13, 28, 35, 12 and 72.

*Beat.*

ROSA: You win?

MARY: No.

ROSA: Sorry.

MARY: You're a baby. How old are you?

ROSA: You're a fossil.

MARY: What?

ROSA: Never mind.

*Mary crosses to the radio and turns it off. Rosa watches.*

MARY: Can you put the knife down. You don't need it.

ROSA: How do you know?

MARY: Seems like you're in trouble enough as it is.

ROSA: Shut up! (beat) Now you sit on the couch – face the wall.

*Beat. Mary stares at Rosa for a moment. She heads to the couch and sits next to the artwork.*

MARY: You see my paintings?

ROSA: You buy them or do them?

MARY: Did 'em.

*Beat.*

ROSA: Face the wall.

MARY: You like 'em?

ROSA: Why? You want a critique?

MARY: You take a look. Tell me what you think and then you can go.

*Beat. Rosa comes around the front of the couch and looks at the paintings.*

ROSA: They're ok. Not great. You're no Georgia O'Keefe. Not bad, though.

MARY: Uh huh.

ROSA: Happy now?

MARY: Yeah. Thanks.

*Beat.*

ROSA: I'm going.

MARY: Be careful, hear?

ROSA: What are you, my mother? I'm sticking a knife in your face!

MARY: You wouldn't use it. (beat) It's cold outside. You cold? You probably hungry.

*Rosa doesn't move. Mary turns to her.*

MARY: You hungry? I'll feed you if you put that knife away.

ROSA: Don't bullshit me.

MARY: If you ain't taking bandages, you might as well have some food. I'll make you a sandwich.

ROSA: Why?

*Beat.*

MARY: It's not every day I get visitors.

> *Beat. Rosa presses the blade into the handle of the knife. She watches Mary as Mary crosses to the kitchen.*

MARY: And if you want to stop that bleeding –

ROSA: I'm all right!

> *Mary shrugs. Starts making a sandwich. Rosa studies the apartment. She crosses to the window and looks out, then moves over to the couch. She looks at the paintings there and pulls out a colorful one: streaks of bright purple, yellow and orange, blue and white. She stares at it for a while.*

ROSA: I like this.

MARY: Don't bullshit me.

ROSA: No. Really.

> *Mary crosses to Rosa with the sandwich. She hands it over, then grabs her pocketbook, removing it from the couch.*

MARY: That's my favorite one. (beat) I'll never do anything better.

> *Rosa takes a bite of her sandwich.*

MARY: You got a name? What's your name?

ROSA: (Mouth full.) Rosa.

MARY: I'm Mary.

*Beat.*

ROSA: Good sandwich, Mary.

MARY: Thanks.

*Long beat.*

MARY: The police after you? (beat) Listen, Rosa – 'sonly a question. Don't I get something in exchange for that sandwich?

ROSA: I said I liked your painting.

MARY: That ain't hardly a fair trade.

ROSA: Tough.

MARY: Don't I get something?

ROSA: You get my company: my sparkling presence.

MARY: Hope that don't mean you'll stay here as long as I feed you.

ROSA: I got places to go. I'm a busy woman.

MARY: Woman?

*Mary laughs. Rosa glares at her.*

MARY: So – the police after you?

ROSA: It's been real, Grandma.

*Rosa gets up to leave.*

MARY: I bet it's cold out there.

ROSA: It's cold everywhere.

*Rosa crosses to the door.*

# Abstract Purple

MARY: There's more food if you still hungry. And them band-aids.

*Rosa smirks at Mary. She grabs the doorknob. Beat. She turns to Mary and the two stare at each other.*

*Lights.*

INTERLUDE

*Lights up on Rosa.*

ROSA: In the dream I'm back in science class, studying this old woman – Mary. That's the assignment. She's in a glass box, with tubes and wires connected to her. She's painting. Not a bad painting, but she's still no Georgia O'Keefe. And Mr. Post, my cute science teacher with the bad breath, is droning on and on about how there are no others left like her. He has this incredible way of making even potentially interesting things boring as shit. So I'm trying to make notes, I have "Old Mary" written at the top of the page, but instead of continuing to write I start yawning and my notes turn into doodles of Mr. Post, moustache and all, and then the moustache grows bigger and bigger and soon the page is just a mass of squiggles and my eyelids are getting heavy, but I can't fall asleep – this is class after all – and my staying awake has a direct bearing on the semester grade, and my grade has a direct bearing on my dad and his "anger issues" and I MUST STAY AWAKE. But my eyes are so heavy – and like the beginning of Charlie Chaplin film, the world flickers between dark and light as I fight sleep. Mary paints. Darkness. Mr. Post. Darkness. My notes. Darkness. I give in to the exhaustion, I know it's all over – life as I know it. There's no going back.

*Lights.*


SCENE TWO

*The morning after. There are a bundle of blankets and pillows in the middle of the room, and an iPod which rests on the counter. Mary sits on the couch, with the LIFE magazine inches from her face.*

*The bundle on the floor stirs. Rosa's face pokes out from under a blanket. She sits up with a start.*

MARY: Morning -

ROSA: Mmm. How -

MARY: Sleep well?

ROSA: How long -

MARY: Musta been tired.

ROSA: How long was I out?

MARY: You still sleep!

ROSA: I'm up Grandma!

MARY: You can still sleep if you want -

ROSA: No. How long was I out? I gotta be going.

MARY: Going? You ain't even awake yet.

ROSA: Well, when I finally wake up I'm heading out.

MARY: You sleep.

ROSA: No! I'm awake! I'm wide awake!

MARY: Sleep more if you want.

ROSA: I'm awake - just stop!

MARY: I was only -

ROSA: I know. Just don't. No demands. No requests. Those are the rules, Grandma, remember? Or do you have trouble remembering? It was much better when you were in the glass box.

MARY: I never been in no glass box.

ROSA: Yeah you were. (beat) Never mind.

   *Beat.*

MARY: You snore you know.

ROSA: Do not.

MARY: Heard ya.

*Beat.*

ROSA: Did I keep you up?

MARY: Nah. Lucky for you I'm mostly deaf.

ROSA: But you could still hear me snore.

MARY: That's how loud you was.

ROSA: I couldn't have been asleep that long. I was watching.

MARY: Well, you was out cold. If you was watching you got pictures on your eyelids.

*Beat.*

ROSA: I'm hungry. How about some breakfast?

MARY: You cooking?

ROSA: You don't cook?

MARY: Nope.

ROSA: How do you eat?

MARY: Don't.

ROSA: Good – all the more food for me.

MARY: Ain't no food.

ROSA: You had groceries yesterday.

MARY: Nothing left. I ate it.

ROSA: Everything – in those bags?

MARY: What was I supposed to do while I was watching you sleep?

ROSA: You were watching me?

MARY: Yeah, so?

ROSA: So, you're just – weird.

MARY: Thank you.

ROSA: Yeah. (beat) I'll buy some stuff. You give me money.

MARY: You don't have no money?

ROSA: I'm the guest, right? Your house, your kitchen, your money.

MARY: Ought to get yourself a job –

ROSA: I don't need a job.

MARY: Why? You a queen or something? (beat) You ain't told me who you are.

ROSA: Rosa.

MARY: Besides that. Why don't you need a job?

ROSA: Because. I got other things.

MARY: Like parents who miss you?

ROSA: Drop it.

MARY: Dropped. You break in places a lot?

ROSA: What are you – Diane Sawyer? At your age, more like Barbara Walters.

MARY: So's just luck brought you to me.

ROSA: That's it.

# Abstract Purple

MARY: And you sure you ain't met before?

ROSA: WILL YOU STOP WITH THE QUESTIONS!

MARY: You want money, you better stop that yelling.

ROSA: Hey Gram, no skin off my butt. I just thought you could use some of my gourmet cooking. I could leave right now.

MARY: I'll give you money.

ROSA: Yeah, you will. Let me use the toilet first.

> *Rosa disappears into the bathroom. She can be heard going through cabinets. Beat. Mary begins going through Rosa's backpack.*

ROSA: (From off.) How long have you been living here?

MARY: About twenty years.

ROSA: How much rent you pay?

> *Mary has found several comic books, a novel, a book of poetry, a calculator, and a small case of tampons in Rosa's bag. She pulls out Rosa's knife and holds it up to the light.*

MARY: Now who's acting like Diane what's-her-name? Ain't you getting a bit personal?

ROSA: About *rent?* I haven't asked you anything personal yet.

> *Rosa can be heard fiddling with the door. Mary shoves all the stuff back in the backpack and zips it up. Rosa re-enters the room. She stares at Mary. Beat.*

MARY: Anything interesting in my medicine chest?

ROSA: Not really. (beat) Why do you live up here anyway?

MARY: What do you mean?

ROSA: It's Harlem. White people up here are up-and-coming. You're neither.

MARY: I live where I wants to live.

*Beat.*

ROSA: You got that money?

*Mary grabs her purse.*

MARY: I think I'm gonna start a new painting.

ROSA: Knock yourself out.

MARY: What's your favorite color?

ROSA: What the hell do you want with me? You watch me when I sleep, ask for a critique of your work, personal information and now – my favorite color? You're crazy. (beat) Mauve. Can I get that cash now?

MARY: Mauve?

ROSA: Purple.

MARY: Oh! That's a good color.

> *Mary has taken an interest in Rosa's iPod. She squints at it, turning it over in her hands. She presses a button. Puts one of the ear-buds up to her ear.*

MARY: You like this music?

> *Rosa shuts the iPod off. Puts it and the ear-buds in her pocket.*

ROSA: I'm hungry.

*She holds out a hand for the money.*

MARY: Here's twenty. Let's write down what we need.

ROSA: Come on, lady – we're not playing house. You're wasting time. I gotta get out of here at a decent hour.

# Abstract Purple

MARY: Why don't you stay a while? You can shop for me and make some of them gourmet meals.

ROSA: Save it Grandma. (beat) The list –

> *Mary gets a pad and starts writing slowly. Throughout, Rosa fidgets impatiently.*

MARY: Eggs, bread, cheese –

ROSA: Gouda. (beat) G-O-U-D-A.

MARY: I can spell.

ROSA: (quickly) Milk, green pepper, parsley, tomato –

MARY: I'm gonna like this stuff?

ROSA: Trust me.

MARY: Hah!

> *Rosa snatches the money and the list.*

MARY: Bring back my change. And get me a lottery ticket. There's a bodega right out –

ROSA: I know where it is.

> *Rosa puts her jacket on and leaves humming.*

> *Mary turns on the radio. Flips through a few stations, trying to find something. She stops at a station with a bouncy pop instrumental playing. Mary nods – she's found music similar to what she heard on the iPod. Mary takes a deep breath, apparently more exhausted than she was letting on when Rosa was in the room. She shuffles over to the closet. She retrieves paint supplies.*

MARY: If that don't beat all. Purple – you're something else – Joseph would have liked you. You got spunk. Really shakes things up – don't it? But it's good.

*She sets up her painting supplies: paint, palette, canvas.*

MARY: How long you been running, child? Slow down, Rosa. Slow down.

*She mixes paint on her palette. Stares at the colored blobs.*

MARY: Purple. Red and blue. Red. (beat) Which one are you? Come on. I can't tell you apart no more.

*She mixes colors at random.*

MARY: Purple!

*She throws the palette down.*

MARY: It's really going. I'm losing it. (beat) Please stay. Help. Maybe if I get sick – Purple – you'll stay then, maybe?

*She goes into the bathroom and can be heard rummaging around in the cabinet. She enters with several pill bottles and a glass of water. She tries to read the labels on each bottle. She begins to drink, turning up the volume on the radio. Mary finishes her water and begins to dance. There's a knock at the door.*

ROSA: Grandma – let me in!

*Mary turns the radio off and starts toward the door. She stops, turning to the mess she made of the pill bottles. Rosa knocks again.*

ROSA: I'm not waiting all day. Come on!

*Mary scoops the pill bottles up. She dumps everything in a drawer. Crosses to the door and opens it. Rosa's holding a bag of groceries.*

ROSA: It's about time.

MARY: You sure came back real fast.

*Rosa puts the groceries down and begins to unpack the bag.*

ROSA: Store is right downstairs. The selection sucks.

MARY: What happened? They run out of Gouda?

ROSA: You were blasting music.

MARY: The loudness got stuck. So - where do you usually shop?

ROSA: Nice try. You know I was thinking about all the stuff you said yesterday about calling the police. You don't even have a phone. I could have robbed you, or worse.

MARY: You still can.

ROSA: I'll keep that in mind. The volume gets stuck on your radio?

MARY: Sometimes.

ROSA: I had a toaster like that once - kept burning toast. There was a trick to it. I'd time it and force it to be done when I was ready. You have to know how to get it to do what you want. Control the thing.

MARY: Control. Ok.

ROSA: You all right?

MARY: Don't tell me you're concerned about me.

ROSA: I won't.

MARY: I'm just fine Purple.

ROSA: Purple?

MARY: Fits don't it? Listen before you go, I have some old paintings I want to hang in here. I need your help.

ROSA: I gotta go after I make this food.

*Rosa finds a pan and a bowl. She takes out her ingredients.*

MARY: You barely been here any time at all. I know – no pressure – no questions. It ain't like I'm trying to keep you here or nothing. Just thought you could use a warm place for a few days.

ROSA: It's not my style to owe people.

MARY: You wouldn't owe me nothing.

ROSA: Liar –

MARY: Don't be rude to me. I'm trying to be nice. You can get out right now.

ROSA: Calm down.

MARY: You help me with hanging my paintings, I'll get calm. Check in the drawer, the third one. There ought to be a hammer.

*Rosa looks at Mary. She stops cooking and opens the drawer.*

ROSA: Yep. Hammer. Happy?

*Beat. She reaches into the drawer and pulls out the pill bottles.*

ROSA: What's this stuff?

MARY: Medicine.

ROSA: All this shit? You sick?

MARY: I don't sleep too good. Arth-ur-itis, Diabetes.

ROSA: That's too bad. (beat) You see a doctor?

MARY: Not in a while.

ROSA: You ought to get one. Geoffrey says –

MARY: He a doctor?

*Beat.*

ROSA: My dad.

# Abstract Purple

MARY: He know where you are?

ROSA: You know enough about me. I gotta get out of here.

> *Rosa takes the pills, goes into the bathroom and slams the door. Beat. Mary rises and grabs the hammer from the kitchen. She hums the tune from the radio and walks toward the bathroom. She stops at the door.*

MARY: You ain't leaving Purple.

> *Mary grabs the hammer with both hands, raises it above her head and brings it down on the doorknob - bending it out of shape. She laughs.*

MARY: Beautiful. Beautiful.

ROSA: Hey, what was that?

> *Rosa tries the door from inside.*

ROSA: I can't get the door open. Are you Ok?

MARY: Beautiful.

ROSA: You locked me in here. You witch! Let me out. I'll break this goddamn door.

> *Mary crosses to the radio and turns it on. Music fills the room. From inside, Rosa can be heard pounding on the door. Mary studies the room.*

ROSA: Let me out of here. Come on. I'm claustrophobic. That means I'm afraid of small spaces. You're a lot stupider than I thought you were. Really dumb for a white woman. Let me out, bitch. You don't know me. I'm an axe murderer! This is against the law. I could sue you so fast - take you for everything - except you're so dirt poor it wouldn't be worth it. You're just like them - want to hold on to me - like some possession. I've had it with shit like this from people like you. You will not keep me. You won't. I got razors in here. I'll slash my wrists. You want to see painting. I'll do the walls over in my blood.

> *Rosa starts to cry. Mary paints purple designs on the door.*

215

MARY: Something about you, Purple. You interesting. Things are real confusing to me. My eyesight is going. I get scared. It's like I'm drowning, Purple. Swimming around in radio announcements and my own stupid thoughts. But I got the feeling that you can stop the ground from sliding out from underneath me. You got something - You remind me I got stuff to find out as old as I am. I just got to be selfish now. It's like those magic and superheroes you got in your bag and in them comic books. I got powers too, you gived 'em to me.

*Mary begins to dance to the music. Rosa bangs on the other side of the door. Mary stops dancing and grabs a broom. She hits the door back.*

MARY: Shut up that noise, girl.

*There is a knock at the door.*

MAN'S VOICE: What's all the noise!

MARY: (To Rosa.) You ain't getting out of there if you keep this up. (To the voice.) It's nothing Sam - just trying to kill me a rat. But I got it cornered now. Thanks for listening out for me.

MAN'S VOICE: I'm always here for you, babe. Mind if I come in for coffee?

MARY: I ain't got none and you know it.

MAN'S VOICE: How about some sugar then?

MARY: You best get outta here.

*The man laughs. We can hear him walk away.*

MARY: (To Rosa.) You glad now? You soon be quiet. You just stay quiet, Purple and this will be over soon.

*Mary returns to her painting, dancing a bit. The lights dim and Mary dances - lost in her experience.*

*Lights.*

SCENE THREE

*Two o'clock the next morning. The apartment is dark. The radio music is still playing. Beyond that, there's the sound of Rosa still struggling with the door. The front door is open. Mary is nowhere to be seen.*

*The bathroom door suddenly swings open. Rosa stands there, exhausted, but triumphant. She quickly collects herself and, after searching for Mary, dashes about the room collecting her possessions. She grabs her jacket and flings her backpack over her shoulder. She reaches the front door and finds it open. Mary can be heard humming as she comes down the hall.*

*Rosa ducks back into the room. She pulls out her knife. Mary enters the room slowly. She is covered in purple paint. As she walks, she holds onto the wall. It becomes obvious that she can no longer see. Rosa is shocked at her appearance at first, then jumps in front of her, holding out her knife. Mary hears the noise and stops.*

MARY: Who's there? Stop. Don't hurt me. (beat) You don't want to hurt an old blind woman. What do you want? Anything you want, if I got it, it's yours.

*Rosa pushes Mary to the couch, forcing her to sit.*

MARY: You want money? I got some. It might take me a while to find it because I'm blind and all. I hate living alone. But I do. I do live alone. Yep. (beat) You still here – ain't ya? (Long beat.) I ain't been through many robberies, but I ain't never heard of one this strange. Sure feel lots better about you robbing me if I knew how I could help you? (beat) You did a good job by choosing me to rob. I'm real cooperative. I ain't violent. I can't even call the police, cause I ain't got no phone. (Mary laughs.) You don't like to laugh, do ya? Yeah, I know your type.

*Rosa grabs some rags from the kitchen.*

MARY: Did you find something you want to take? Just go on and help yourself.

*Rosa begins to tie Mary's feet together.*

217

MARY: Oh, God - you're tying me up.

*Rosa begins to tie Mary's hands together.*

MARY: I ain't planning to die just yet. If you just come to murder me - I ain't interested. I ain't dying - not after all this work is done. Now that I got me something. Please, untie me -

*Rosa grabs Mary's hair. Mary begins to cry.*

MARY: At least let her see what I done. Let her see. It's all for her. Please.

*Beat. Rosa rises and crosses to the light switch. She turns the lights on. All over the room - in every corner, on every inch of wall and ceiling there is a breathtaking abstract painting. There are streaks of purple - different shades, designs. It is intricate, phenomenal.*

ROSA: Oh my god.

MARY: Purple? You scared the wits outta me, child. (beat) It's your gift.

ROSA: The ceiling is so high. You couldn't have gotten all the corners.

MARY: You gave me so much. A long time ago I used to do portraits. But it was never right. But I kept on: "Joseph. Sit, please." He was such a beautiful brown man. He'd sit and it wouldn't get no better. Something would be different every time - something I wouldn't get. The curve of his mouth - the glow in his eyes. I kept working on it. And then - I did it. I finally captured my Joseph on paper. He had the littlest, cutest ears, my Joseph. (beat) When he passed on it only seemed right. Couldn't be in two places at once. I'd trapped his spirit. (beat) Stopped drawing after that. I'd only paint - make up shapes and forms. (beat) Recently started giving up on stuff. And I began my first portrait since Joseph. It was a picture of me. I stopped it the day you came. You just run in here bouncin' and swingin' that knife all over the place. Like you could take on anything. I been smiling inside ever since. This painting came outta that smile - just like that. It's like I captured you better in this abstract painting than any of the greatest portrait painters coulda done. (beat) You free to go now that I gave you this.

*Beat.*

# Abstract Purple

ROSA: You really pushed yourself to the limit for this. But it's hardly worth the shit you put me through. You did this for yourself. Not me. You don't know me.

> *Rosa grabs her stuff. She begins to fill her backpack with food from the kitchen. Then she takes more money from Mary's purse.*

MARY: What're you doing?

ROSA: Stocking for my trip.

MARY: Rosa –

ROSA: Purple to you. Fits right? You don't want to get to know me – to really know me. You don't care about me. You proved that when you broke that doorknob.

MARY: I tried to know you. You never told me about yourself. I asked you.

ROSA: I've got to get home.

MARY: Home? How'm I supposed to get out of these once you leave?

ROSA: That's not my problem.

MARY: Guess not. You just want to come in here like you're some princess. Pull a knife on me and all that – and don't expect me to do nothing? You ought to be grateful.

ROSA: That you locked me in the bathroom?

MARY: I wanted to keep you here because – I liked you. I wanted you around. You give me my energy back. I thought I was dying, but I'm not – And when they come and cart my dead body outta here – they'll look around and – they'll think something nice about me – about what I've done. And you did it as much as me. You give me this feeling and I gave you something back. So just go on and leave me here. You just go and don't think about what I done give you. Maybe I ain't all there. But I ain't hurt you or nothing. I just wanted to hold on.

ROSA: You're too interested in holding on to see who you're holding on to.

MARY: No. You're wrong there. I saw you - I watched you. In spite of yourself. I listened to your music - I studied you as best I could. I saw you scared and alone - lost and angry. You're just like me. You can't tell me no different. I saw you. You were the last thing I saw clearly. You just give this painting a long look. You'll see how much I saw you.

*Rosa finishes gathering her stuff.*

MARY: You just gonna leave me here, without saying nothing else? That whole time you were in there - I didn't eat nothing. You leave me like this, I'll starve. Please, Purple. Ain't you gonna untie me? I been trying my damnedest to help. You never let me in. Look at what I done.

ROSA: I've seen enough.

MARY: You ain't seen nothing. I know you. What you probably did was like glancing at the Sistine Chapel. I'm offended.

ROSA: You think I care, after what you did?

MARY: No I guess you don't. I don't blame you - after all you been through. Not that I know what you been through, cause you ain't told me. But you musta suffered a whole lot. And you must be starving too. How about you make us breakfast before you go?

ROSA: Forget it.

MARY: I'm hungry.

ROSA: You should have thought of that before.

MARY: You're right. Once again.

ROSA: Besides you left this food out all night. Everything I bought is spoiled. You're crazy. You're a sick old woman. I gotta go. Even if I wanted to, I couldn't make anything out of this. My dog wouldn't even eat this crap.

MARY: What kind of dog?

ROSA: Amigo is a sheepdog.

MARY: You Spanish?

ROSA: Probably the first preppie Hispanic you ever saw. (beat) I'm adopted. My folks are white.

MARY: That why you ran away?

ROSA: No. Yeah. It's a long story.

MARY: I ain't going nowhere.

> *Beat.*

ROSA: I don't know. It's stupid. I - sometimes I think they're too busy for me. That all they like to do is show me off at parties, brag about my grades and how well-adjusted I am. Like they're better white people for having adopted someone of a different race. I get tired of feeling - so unique - like not in a teenage way, but in a real way. I'm tired of it. And my dad, he has all these problems - gets really angry when I get sad. And I get sad a lot. (beat) I start thinking that I'm lost. Feeling it. It's sorta like we all want the perfect family. And we're mad that we're not it.

> *Beat.*

MARY: What's perfect anyway? (beat) Where's your real folks?

ROSA: Don't know. Don't know anything about my real parents. I don't know anything about being Hispanic. I'm tired of being a freak. We had a big fight the other day. Big. And I took off. But I guess they really care about me: they never locked me in the bathroom.

MARY: It's hard when you're lost to yourself.

ROSA: How do you know?

MARY: There was a time when I wasn't exactly among my own up here. But I belong all the same. You'll find you do too. You'll figure out how you fit in - even if you can't see it now. (beat) So, what did you fight about?

ROSA: Everything. You don't want to hear this.

MARY: Don't tell me what I want to hear.

ROSA: I gotta go.

MARY: No you don't. Not before you take a damn good look at my painting.

> *Beat. Rosa looks at Mary.*

MARY: Rosa?

ROSA: Yeah?

MARY: You was quiet and I thought you was gonna leave me like this.

ROSA: I was thinking about what you said. About belonging.

MARY: I'm right, too.

ROSA: Maybe.

MARY: No, Purple. I am. (beat) But then I'm right most of the time.

> *Rosa smiles. She takes a long slow look around at the painting as the lights fade.*


INTERLUDE

> *Lights up on Rosa in the dream space.*

ROSA: In the dream, everybody I ever met is standing in a prison cell. But it looks like Mary's apartment. It's crowded. Packed. Just enough room for me before the next person. There's a therapist somewhere, but no one can find him – or her. I guess it's supposed to be a group session. With a really large group. My science teacher is there and mom and dad, Mary and me and everyone from school – even Catherine Maxwell, who hates my guts. I hate hers too. But for some reason, the room is warm and no one minds being shoved up against each other. Then I start to panic. My breath gets shallow and I start to think about why we're here: if we're waiting out a nuclear war or if we're suffering through some kind of purgatory, or if the therapy session will ever begin. But the moment passes and someone behind me starts to laugh. And through all those people – all those bodies pressed together – I can feel the laughter. Pretty soon everyone is laughing. And it's like – it's not a prison at all. It's a party. Without music and dancing, 'cause there's no room. It's a party. We talk together. We smile together. We breathe together.

> *Lights fade.*

## SCENE FOUR

> *St. Nicholas Park. Two months later.*

> *Rosa stands. She is holding a book of poetry. Mary is seated on a bench with a sketch pad on her lap. They are both wearing winter coats. Rosa reads.*

ROSA: "I exist as I am, and that is enough.
If no other in the world be aware, I sit content.
And if each and all are aware, I sit content.
One world is aware, and by far the largest to me
and that is myself."

MARY: That's beautiful.

ROSA: Whitman is my favorite.

MARY: What's it called?

ROSA: Song of Myself.

MARY: Read the first part over again.

ROSA: No. I've read the whole poem twice already.

> *They laugh.*

MARY: What time is it?

ROSA: Four-thirty. My dad will be here soon.

MARY: I'm glad you're getting along better.

ROSA: Yeah, it's OK. Therapy helps. And it's good they let me do some things I want to do. Like visit you. Still, they can be annoying.

MARY: Give 'em time, Rosa. Some people are slow learners.

*They laugh.*

ROSA: Guess what?

MARY: Uh oh. (beat) Every time you say that - you done brought me a surprise. Now I like the iPod and all that music. And the computer. And the groceries. But good God, you done enough -

ROSA: Not yet. (beat) Don't you want to know what it is?

MARY: No. Jus' take it back. I mean it.

ROSA: Ok. You're right. (beat) It was Dad's idea anyway.

MARY: Take it back.

ROSA: Him.

MARY: You got me a man? You're giving me your daddy?

ROSA: No.

MARY: Then what "him"? No don't tell me. No, tell me.

ROSA: No, we'll take him back.

MARY: Oh my - you didn't get me a seeing eye dog, did you?

ROSA: Not if you don't want him.

MARY: Oh, my - Joseph, you hear that? This girl and her family done gone crazy! Of course I want that dog. What kind? What's he look like? Is he toilet trained?

ROSA: He flushes and everything.

# Abstract Purple

MARY: You know what I mean.

ROSA: I can't tell you about him because it's supposed to be a secret. You can't tell Dad I told you. If it's not the perfect surprise you'll undo all the progress we've made in family therapy.

MARY: Ok.

ROSA: You promise?

MARY: Yeah. Can't wait 'till he gets here though.

ROSA: You better act natural.

MARY: Read me that poem again.

ROSA: Mary!

> *Mary picks up her charcoals. She feels along the box to select the right colors.*

MARY: Let's get back to my drawing. What's going on now?

> *As Rosa talks, she resumes drawing.*

ROSA: The snow is real soft looking. The trees and branches are covered. Crystal blankets. Soft. Sparkling.

MARY: Is it getting dark?

ROSA: A little. The snow is taking on the mauve tint of the sky. Kinda purple. The trees look like hands: reaching fingers. Frozen. Black silhouettes. And there are people walking by, holding hands. (beat) I'm scared for you. I wish I could help you see again.

MARY: I'm happy. Glad you came to visit.

ROSA: I like taking care of you, describing colors to you.

MARY: You do a good job.

ROSA: You done yet?

MARY: Just about.

*Mary finishes. She hands Rosa the sketch pad. Beat.*

MARY: What's it look like?

ROSA: You sure you can't see?

*They laugh.*

*Blackout.*

FINAL INTERLUDE

*Lights up on Rosa. She's smiling.*

ROSA: In the dream I am running through the park - toward her. Laughing as she describes the colors of my outfit, and of the world around me. She changes the descriptions and the colors really change. There are times I remember how it was, and I run my hands along the scars from the monster's last attack. But I'm healing. There are times when I'm afraid, but the monster isn't here - this is someplace else. It's not exactly new or old, but kind of - both. Eternal. Ordinary. Realistic. Abstract. I don't know. Sometimes my therapist is in the dream. Sometimes my parents. But Mary is always there, and the paintings. I know the fear won't disappear completely. But even wide awake I can't hold on to the feeling. The images, the thoughts, the colors seem to shift and change in magnificent patterns.

*Blackout.*

*End of play.*

# A FEW SHORT PLAYS: PERFORMANCE HISTORY

## First Encounter [2005]

First Encounter was performed at the NBC Universal Diversity Scene Showcase at The Falcon Theater in Burbank, CA in 2005. Directed by Somnath Sen with Yasmine Dalawari and Len Cordova.


## Many Happy Returns [2020]

Many Happy Returns was performed online in 2020 at New Jersey's Vivid Stage (then called Dreamcatcher Repertory Theater) in an evening called Holiday Bites. Directed by Laura Ekstrand with Neimah Djourabchi, Harriett Trangucci, Darin Earl and Jean Goto.


## This is Now [2005]

This is Now was performed at The American Airlines Theater in an evening for the 24 Hour Plays on Broadway (a benefit for Working Playground) in 2005. It was directed by Mary Kate Burke with Tracie Thoms, Wilson Jermaine Heredia, Margaret Colin, William Sadler and Hayden Christensen.


## Iggie Imagines Marriage [1996]

Iggie Imagines Marriage was first performed at The John Houseman Studio in 1996 as part of an evening called Random Acts of Love, produced by Stephanie and Alan Mittman, Mark Rennie and Sanford Schimel. It was directed by Kevin Sturtevant with Michael Cavalier and Ron Bopst. The play debuted professionally at New Jersey's Vivid Stage (then called Dreamcatcher Repertory Theater) in 2001 as part of an evening called Love, Hate, Friendship, Marriage. It was directed by Laura Ekstrand with Harry Patrick Christian and Jeff Stone.

## Like the End of the World [2009]

Like the End of the World was commissioned by PJ Paparelli for The American Theater Company in Chicago as part of The Silver Project in 2010. It was directed by Jeffrey Stanton with Steven Royce Stinson, Jonathan Verge and Ebony Wimbs.

## Three People [2020]

Three People was presented online as part of While We Breathe, a digital protest produced by Arvind Ethan David and Sean Chia. It was directed by Steve Harper with Keith Eric Chappelle and Burgundi Baker.

## Actual Cost [2006]

Actual Cost was performed at the Juilliard 100th Anniversary Celebration in an evening called Ten times Ten in 2006. It was directed by Will Pomerantz with Erica B. Peeples, Jimmy Davis and JaMario Stills.

## Special Counsel [2017]

Special Counsel was performed in 2018 at New Jersey's Vivid Stage (then called Dreamcatcher Repertory Theater) which also commissioned the play as part of an evening called Continuing the Conversation. It was directed by Jessica O'Hara-Baker with Gary-Kayi Fletcher, Beth Painter, Michael Aquino, Amanda Salazar and Noreen Farley.

## 21st Century Tactics [2016]

21st Century Tactics was presented in 2016 at New Jersey's Vivid Stage (then called Dreamcatcher Repertory Theater) which also commissioned the play as part of an evening called Continuing the Conversation. It was directed by Alex Craig Mann with Jason Szamreta and Porché Hardy.

## The Political Machine [2020]

The Political Machine was commissioned by L.A.'s Lower Depth Theater Ensemble and presented online as part of an evening entitled The BIPOC Voting Plays in 2020. It was directed by Gregg Daniel with Gilbert Glenn Brown, Yvonne Huff Lee and Tasha Ames.

## A Few Short Plays to Save the World [2018]

A Few Short Plays to Save the World was presented online in 2021 through Northwestern University's Wirtz Center. It was directed by Tor Campbell with Jarris Al'Jaleel Mchee, Jasmine Sharma, Jared Son and Bennett Petersen.

## What You Did [2016]

What You Did was presented online in 2021 through Northwestern University's Wirtz Center. It was directed by Tor Campbell with Jarris Al'Jaleel Mchee, Jasmine Sharma, Jared Son and Bennett Petersen.

## How to Teach the Civil War [2012]

How to Teach the Civil War was presented at The Writers Guild of America West as part of the Committee of Black Writers' event The Black Scene in 2017. The play was directed by Steve Harper with Hansford Prince, Tiffany Black and David Thomas Jenkins.

## Abstract Purple [1990]

Abstract Purple was performed at the Fells Point Corner Theater as part of the Baltimore Playwrights Festival in 1994. It was directed by Miriam Bazensky with JoAnna Lynn Senatore and Anne B. Mulligan.

# ACKNOWLEDGMENTS

Thanks first, to my parents, whose respect for the arts allowed me the space to put words on the page – even allowing me to write poems at the dinner table when the Muse was calling. (That sounds really annoying but I think it only happened once.) To every playwriting teacher I ever had, those who believed in me enough to cheer me on and those who didn't. I received enough wisdom and sustenance to keep at it – and that's all anyone could ever really ask for. Thanks, too, to those fellow writers out there who I've bumped into and up against – who have challenged and celebrated me – directly or by example. You make me want to be better than I am. Outside of a gaggle of coaches, therapists, and mentors (you know who you are), I have gratitude to everyone who has read these plays (and all those who helped bring them to life). You taught me a ton about what works and what doesn't and kept me reaching for the sometimes bizarre, sometimes difficult moments that live in my head and echo my experience – and apparently the experiences of many others. Particular thanks to these encouragers: Laura Ekstrand, Kelley Macmillan, Sanford Schimel, John Schwartz, PJ Papparelli, Chris Till, Chris Durang, Marsha Norman, Charles Fuller, Joe Kraemer, Tina Fallon, Arvind Ethan Davis, Sean Chia, P.A. Skantze, Cezar Williams, Cynthia Robinson, Bob Scanlan, Tor Campbell, Gregg Daniel, Ty Jones and Russell G. Jones. Thanks bell hooks for embracing all of me. Thank you Sandra Daley-Sharif for the encouragement to do this particular collection. Special thanks to those who helped put this book together – chief among them Shawn René Graham, who is wise, talented, and kind in what she says and what she doesn't say and is always super-easy to work with. Thanks to Sean Cameron for his expertise and humor and Jamil O'Quinn and Ashley Bower for their able assistance. Finally, I wouldn't be complete without sincere thanks to the Great Creator – the voice of inspiration and editing from the Universe. And the voice of kindness. Without you I'm nothing.

Cheers to all those I haven't met and may never meet who read these pages – particularly the outsiders, the queer ones, those who are "different" in skin tone, style, and/or philosophy. I hope you find something useful here. Above all, this is for you: to light your way, give you something to read or perform or direct or reflect on and make you feel a little less weird and lonely. I hope that for all of us. Always.

# ABOUT THE AUTHOR

STEVE HARPER was born in Brooklyn, NY and currently lives in Los Angeles. He is a playwright, TV writer, producer and actor who writes about the "invisible things" (like race, sexuality, politics and religion) that people don't usually talk about. His full-length plays include *Black Lives / Blue Lives* [co-written with Bill Mesce, Jr.] (The Theater Project, NJ), *Urban Rabbit Chronicles* (Georgia Southern University), *Princeton Theory*, *Almost*, and *The Escape Artist's Children*. Readings and workshops: Classical Theatre of Harlem, Lower Depth Theater Ensemble, Celebration Theatre, Malibu Playhouse, Vivid Stage, Roundhouse Theater, Northwestern University, Loyola Marymount University, New York Stage & Film and New York Theatre Workshop.

Steve served as Co-Executive Producer for the CW series *Stargirl*. He's written for *God Friended Me*, *Tell Me Your Secrets*, *American Crime* and *Covert Affairs*. His web series *SEND ME*, about time traveling black people, garnered a 2016 Emmy Nomination for series lead Tracie Thoms (Now on YouTube). Steve's acting work spans TV, film, theater, commercials and voice overs. Awards and honors include a selection as a semi-finalist for the O'Neill Theater Center, the Artistic Achievement Award from the Afro-American Cultural Center at Yale, the Millennium Telly Award, a Weissberger Award nomination, two grants from Lincoln Center's Lecomte Du Nuoy Foundation, a MacDowell National Endowment for the Arts Fellowship and two Yaddo fellowships. He is a graduate of Yale, the A.R.T. Institute at Harvard and the Juilliard playwriting program. He also coaches professional and aspiring writers.

Follow him on Twitter: @harpercreates and @yourcreatvlife. For more information: www.harpercreates.com

Steve is represented by Ally Shuster, Creative Artists Agency, 405 Lexington Avenue, 19th Floor, New York NY 10174 (212) 277-9000, ally.shuster@caa.com.